Guru Guru Pon-Chan 2

Satomi Ikezawa

Translated and adapted by Douglas Varenas

Lettering and touchup by Steve Palmer

BALLANTINE BOOKS • NEW YORK

Guru Guru Pon-Chan 2 is a work of fiction. Names, characters, places, and incidents are the products of the author's imagination or are used fictitiously. Any resemblance to actual events, locales, or persons, living or dead, is entirely coincidental.

2005 Del Rey® Trade Paperback Edition

Published in the United States by Del Rey Books, an imprint of The Random House Publishing Group, a division of Random House, Inc., New York.

First published in Japan in 1998 by Kodansha Ltd., Tokyo,

Library of Congress Control Number: 2005924891

ISBN 0-345-48096-1

Printed in the United States of America

www.delreymanga.com

First Edition

1 3 5 7 9 8 6 4 2

Text design by Steve Palmer

TOMARE!
STOP!!
YOU'RE GOING THE WRONG WAY!
MANGA IS A COMPLETELY DIFFERENT TYPE OF READING EXPERIENCE
TO START AT THE BEGINNING, GO TO THE END!
THAT'S RIGHT! AUTHENTIC MANGA IS READ THE TRADITIONAL JAPANESE WAY—FROM RIGHT TO LEFT. EXACTLY THE OPPOSITE OF HOW AMERICAN BOOKS ARE READ. IT'S EASY TO FOLLOW: JUST GO TO THE OTHER END OF THE BOOK, AND READ EACH PAGE—AND EACH PANEL—FROM THE RIGHT SIDE TO THE LEFT SIDE, STARTING AT THE TOP RIGHT. NOW YOU'RE EXPERIENCING MANGA AS IT WAS MEANT TO BE.

VOLUME 3

BY TOMOKO NINOMIYA

MUSICAL DISSONANCE

Ages: 16 +

Student prodigy Shinichi Chiaki just can't shake Nodame, no matter how hard he tries. Now he is forced to tutor her and Mine all night. So much for music being comforting!

Then Shinichi gets a golden opportunity: the chance to temporarily fill in for Maestro Stresemann as conductor for the S orchestra. But after an unfortunate mishap, the maestro defects to the A orchestra and challenges Shinichi to a public-performance duel. With only weeks to prepare, can members of the inexperienced S orchestra pull themselves together to rival the confidence of the A orchestra? It's going to take a lot of hard work—and inspiration from a certain free-spirited girl with a crush. The battle Shinichi can't afford to lose has begun!

Includes special extras after the story!

VOLUME 3: On sale November 29, 2005!

For more information and to sign up for Del Rey's manga e-newsletter, visit www.delreymanga.com

Contents

A Note from the Author

As her love for Mirai-Kun grows, Ponta's demeanor is becoming more and more woman-like, and she's already changed so much from the beginning of Volume 1. This goes beyond my expectations for Ponta, but I mean that in a good way. By the way, my Pon-Chan and Guts are in the prime of their manhood (they're around 30 years old in human years) but they don't know what it is to love yet. I wonder if they want to love...?

Honorifics

Throughout the Del Rey Manga books, you will find Japanese honorifics left intact in the translations. For those not familiar with how the Japanese use honorifics, and more importantly, how they differ from American honorifics, we present this brief overview.

Politeness has always been a critical facet of Japanese culture. Ever since the feudal era, when Japan was a highly stratified society, use of honorifics–which can be defined as polite speech that indicates relationship or status–has played an essential role in the Japanese language. When addressing someone in Japanese, an honorific usually takes the form of a suffix attached to one's name (example: "Asuna-san"), or as a title at the end of one's name or in place of the name itself (example: "Negi-sensei," or simply "Sensei!").

Honorifics can be expressions of respect or endearment. In the context of manga and anime, honorifics give insight into the nature of the relationship between characters. Many translations into English leave out these important honorifics, and therefore distort the "feel" of the original Japanese. Because Japanese honorifics contain nuances that English honorifics lack, it is our policy at Del Rey not to translate them. Here, instead, is a guide to some of the honorifics you may encounter in Del Rey Manga.

-san: This is the most common honorific, and is equivalent to Mr., Miss, Ms., Mrs., etc. It is the all-purpose honorific and can be used in any situation where politeness is required.

-sama: This is one level higher than "-san." It is used to confer great respect.

-dono: This comes from the word "tono," which means "lord." It is even a higher level than "-sama," and confers utmost respect.

-kun: This suffix is used at the end of boys' names to express familiarity or endearment. It is also sometimes used by men among friends, or when addressing someone younger or of a lower station.

-chan: This is used to express endearment, mostly towards girls. It is also used for little boys, pets, and even among lovers. It gives a sense of childish cuteness.

Bozu: This is an informal way to refer to a boy, similar to the English term "kid" or "squirt."

Sempai: This title suggests that the addressee is one's "senior" in a group or organization. It is most often used in a school setting, where underclassmen refer to their upperclassmen as "sempai." It can also be used in the workplace, such as when a newer employee addresses an employee who has seniority in the company.

Kohai: This is the opposite of "sempai," and is used towards underclassmen in school or newcomers in the workplace. It connotes that the addressee is of lower station.

Sensei: Literally meaning "one who has come before," this title is used for teachers, doctors, or masters of any profession or art.

Anesan: "Anesan" (or "nesan") is a generic term for a girl, usually older, meaning "sister."

Ojou-sama: "Ojou-sama" is a way of referring to the daughter or sister of someone with high political or social status.

-[blank]: Usually forgotten in these lists, but perhaps the most significant difference between Japanese and English. The lack of honorific means that the speaker has permission to address the person in a very intimate way. Usually, only family, spouses, or very close friends have this kind of permission. Known as *yobisute*, it can be gratifying when someone who has earned the intimacy starts to call one by one's name without an honorific. But when that intimacy hasn't been earned, it can also be very insulting.

CHAPTER
NUMBER
5
THE BEST CHRISTMAS
Guru Guru
Pon-Chan
2
Satomi Ikezawa

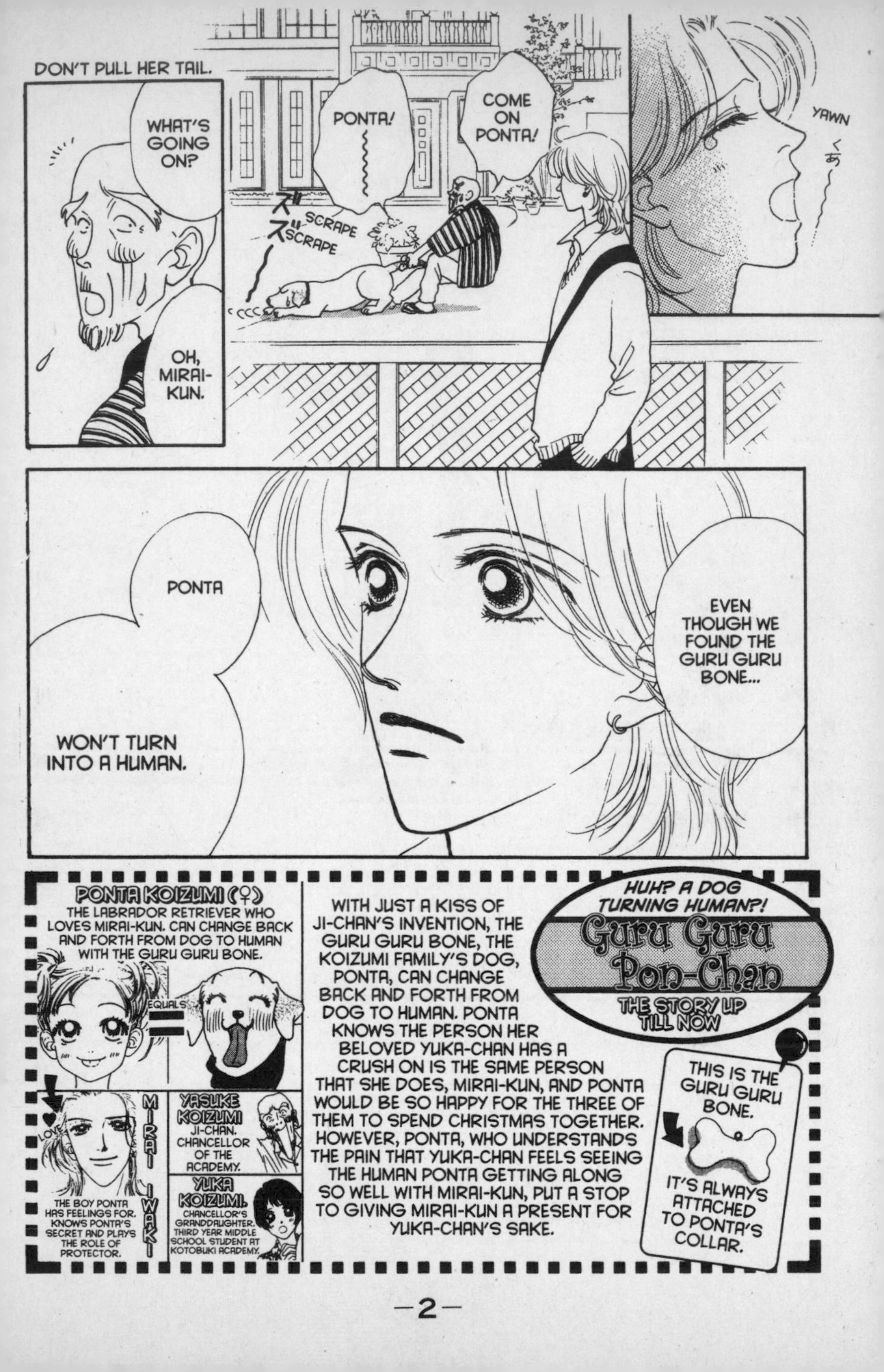

YAWN
COME ON PONTA!
PONTA!
SCRAPE
SCRAPE
DON'T PULL HER TAIL.
WHAT'S GOING ON?
OH, MIRAI-KUN.
EVEN THOUGH WE FOUND THE GURU GURU BONE...
PONTA
WON'T TURN INTO A HUMAN.
HUH? A DOG TURNING HUMAN?!
Guru Guru Pon-Chan
THE STORY UP TILL NOW
WITH JUST A KISS OF JI-CHAN'S INVENTION, THE GURU GURU BONE, THE KOIZUMI FAMILY'S DOG, PONTA, CAN CHANGE BACK AND FORTH FROM DOG TO HUMAN. PONTA KNOWS THE PERSON HER BELOVED YUKA-CHAN HAS A CRUSH ON IS THE SAME PERSON THAT SHE DOES, MIRAI-KUN, AND PONTA WOULD BE SO HAPPY FOR THE THREE OF THEM TO SPEND CHRISTMAS TOGETHER. HOWEVER, PONTA, WHO UNDERSTANDS THE PAIN THAT YUKA-CHAN FEELS SEEING THE HUMAN PONTA GETTING ALONG SO WELL WITH MIRAI-KUN, PUT A STOP TO GIVING MIRAI-KUN A PRESENT FOR YUKA-CHAN'S SAKE.
THIS IS THE GURU GURU BONE.
IT'S ALWAYS ATTACHED TO PONTA'S COLLAR.
PONTA KOIZUMI (♀)
THE LABRADOR RETRIEVER WHO LOVES MIRAI-KUN. CAN CHANGE BACK AND FORTH FROM DOG TO HUMAN WITH THE GURU GURU BONE.
EQUALS
LOVE
MIRAI IWAKI
THE BOY PONTA HAS FEELINGS FOR. KNOWS PONTA'S SECRET AND PLAYS THE ROLE OF PROTECTOR.
YASUKE KOIZUMI
JI-CHAN. CHANCELLOR OF THE ACADEMY.
YUKA KOIZUMI.
CHANCELLOR'S GRANDDAUGHTER. THIRD YEAR MIDDLE SCHOOL STUDENT AT KOTOBUKI ACADEMY.

WHAT'S GOTTEN INTO YOU, PONTA?
NOD NOD
コク コク
どろーん…
WHITHER
LET'S GO TO SCHOOL!
LOOKS LIKE A SERIOUS ILLNESS.
DID SOME-THING HAPPEN?
I DON'T KNOW.

MAYBE SOMETHING BAD HAPPENED TO HER WHEN SHE WAS HUMAN.
YOU BETTER GET GOING, MIRAI-KUN. YOU'LL BE LATE.
YUKA!
YOU GET A MOVE ON TOO, YUKA.
AH
O-OKAY.
YOU TWO TAKE CARE.
YUKA-CHAN...
I HOPE YOU CAN SPEND CHRISTMAS WITH MIRAI-KUN.
I HOPE YOU GIVE HIM...
THAT PRESENT.
I ALSO...

Merry X'mas
WANT TO GIVE THIS TO MIRAI-KUN.
BUT—
YUKA-CHAN, WHO I LOVE SO MUCH...
IT WAS PAINFUL!
TO SEE THE HUMAN PONTA AND MIRAI-KUN GETTING ALONG SO WELL.
IT'S MY FAULT I MADE HER CRY.
I WON'T LET THAT HAPPEN AGAIN.
SO I'M GIVING UP
ON BECOMING HUMAN.
I'M ALSO
GIVING UP... ON LOVE.

211
2-1
I THINK PONTA'S 'COLD' IS PRETTY FISHY.
PERHAPS SHE'S STUDYING FOR FINALS AT HOME?
AFTER ALL, THEY SAY SHE'S A RETURNEE
HA HA HA
I DON'T THINK THAT'S THE CASE. A DOG'S PAW CAN'T HOLD A PENCIL.
WHAT ?! CAN'T HOLD A PENCIL ?!
NOW I'VE DONE IT.
IT'S NOTHING. NEVER MIND.
MIRAI-KUUUN
EVEN THOUGH IT'S TIRING, I WISH SHE WAS HERE...
RATTLE
KOIZUMI

PON-CHAN
....

I'VE GOT IT!! THIS YEAR'S CHRISTMAS...
WE'LL HAVE A BIG HOUSE PARTY WITH THE WHOLE FAMILY!!
H...
HOUSE PARTY ~~~?

WE HAVEN'T HAD A PARTY AT THE HOUSE IN THE LONGEST TIME.
I LIKE TO HAVE THEM FROM TIME TO TIME.
THEN IT'S DECIDED!
WHOO HOO!
BUT THEN, WHAT ABOUT CHRISTMAS WITH MIRAI-KUN?
YUKA-CHAN......?
LET'S COOK TOGETHER, MAMA!
Y-YEAH.
LEAVE THE TREE TO ME!!
WHAT ABOUT THE PRESENT?
YUKA-CHAN—?

WHAT?! YOU'RE GONNA PASS?
BUT WE'RE HAVING A KARAOKE CHRISTMAS PARTY.
SORRY. I'M HAVING A PARTY AT MY HOUSE.
I'VE GOT TO GET READY, SO I'LL SEE YOU LATER.
WHAT?! YOU'RE WORKING?
CAN'T YOU CALL IN SICK?
I CAN'T DO THAT.
THAT'S RIGHT
BUT IT'S CHRISTMAS EVE! CHRISTMAS!

フラワー
EVERYONE LIKES CHRISTMAS.
I WONDER IF SANTA WILL COME?
ROAST CHICKEN 250 YEN*.
*ABOUT $3
TOYS
HOW ABOUT ASKING SANTA?
YEAH
WOW!
IT LOOKS DELICIOUS ~ ♡
OKAY THEN, CAN YOU MAKE THE SALAD?
OKAY.
I'M GOING TO BUY THE CHAMPAGNE
CHOP
CHOP
CHOP
UMM, CELERY, CELERY.

!!!
PO-PO-PON-CHAN! THAT'S DANGEROUS!
はん
STUN
HEY, SHOULD YOU BE HAVING THIS PARTY?!
WEREN'T YOU GOING TO SPEND CHRISTMAS WITH MIRAI-KUN?!
UH...
IT'S EVEN MORE DANGEROUS TO SNATCH FOOD.
YUKA-CHAN.
TRAMP TRAMP

THAT'S NOT HAPPENING.
WE DECIDED TO HAVE A PARTY AT HOME TODAY
SO I'M FINE WITH THAT!
OKAY THEN, WE'VE GOT TO MAKE THIS SALAD QUICK
HER EXPRESSION...
IT TELLS A DIFFERENT STORY. YUKA-CHAN!
I QUIT BECOMING HUMAN FOR YUKA-CHAN'S SAKE.

THIS TIME FOR YUKA-CHAN'S SAKE...
PON-CHAN...
YUKA-CHAN...
COME WITH ME.
I'LL BECOME HUMAN.
PONTA?!
BANZAI! BANZAI!
THE HUMAN PONTA HAS MADE A COMEBACK!

WAIT HERE.
WHAT'S GOTTEN INTO YOU ALL OF A SUDDEN, PO...?
WAIT, YUKA-CHAN.
PON-CHAN!

PLEASE WAIT, OKAY YUKA-CHAN?
WHAT'S WRONG WITH THAT GIRL?
A-AN ALLIGATOR GIRL
SNIFF SNIFF
くんくんくん
SNIFF SNIFF SNIFF
DON'T MOVE A MUSCLE. WAIT.
...
THIS ISN'T EASY TO DO IN THIS BODY
SMOOTCH
ちゅぱッ
JEEZ, WHAT A BOTHER.
SUZUKI GARDEN
SALE!
SALE!
TODAY'S THE DAY SO DON'T MISS OUT.
HOW ABOUT A TREE, MA'AM?!
THANK YOU
RUSTLE
HEY, WHAT DO YOU THINK YOU'RE DOING?

T-THIEF!
PONTA!
DASH
WAIT!
THAT'S STORE MERCHANDISE!
STOP MESSING AROUND!
GOOD GIRL. NOW GIVE IT BACK...
NO WAY!
THE "INVITATION TO PLAY" POSE
COIL
AT TIMES, IT'S ALSO MERELY 'STRETCHING'.

ARE YOU TRYING TO PISS ME OFF?!
♪
SPRING
WHEEZE, WHEEZE, JUST A SEC, PONTA.
WAIT FOR ME, WHEEZE.
COME ON NOW!
WHEEZE, WHEEZE, I CAN'T GO ON.
....

HAH! I WAS LYING!
OOH HAH HAH HAH
KYA!
CLUNK
...
I'M SERIOUS, NO MERCY NOW!
KYA! KYA! KYA!
WOW, RIGHT NOW...
I'M HAVING THE BEST CHRISTMAS.

THE BEST CHRISTMAS...
WITH JUST ME AND THE ONE I LOVE.
......
RUSTLE
TRAMP TRAMP
PON-CHAN!
HUH?
WHY'D YOU BECOME A DOG?
AND WHAT'S THIS LACE ALL ABOUT?

MI-MIRAI.
HI.
I DON'T KNOW WHAT THIS IS ALL ABOUT BUT...
PON-CHAN, WHAT'S GOING ON?
AH!
WHAT'RE YOU DOING ?!
PONTA ?!
ROMP
ROMP
PON-CHAN!
ZIP
WHAT WAS SHE THINKING ?!
AH, I'LL UNTANGLE US.
O...
OKAY.
PON-CHAN
PITTER
PATTER
MY PLAN FROM THE START WAS TO MEET MIRAI-SAN...
PITTER
PATTER

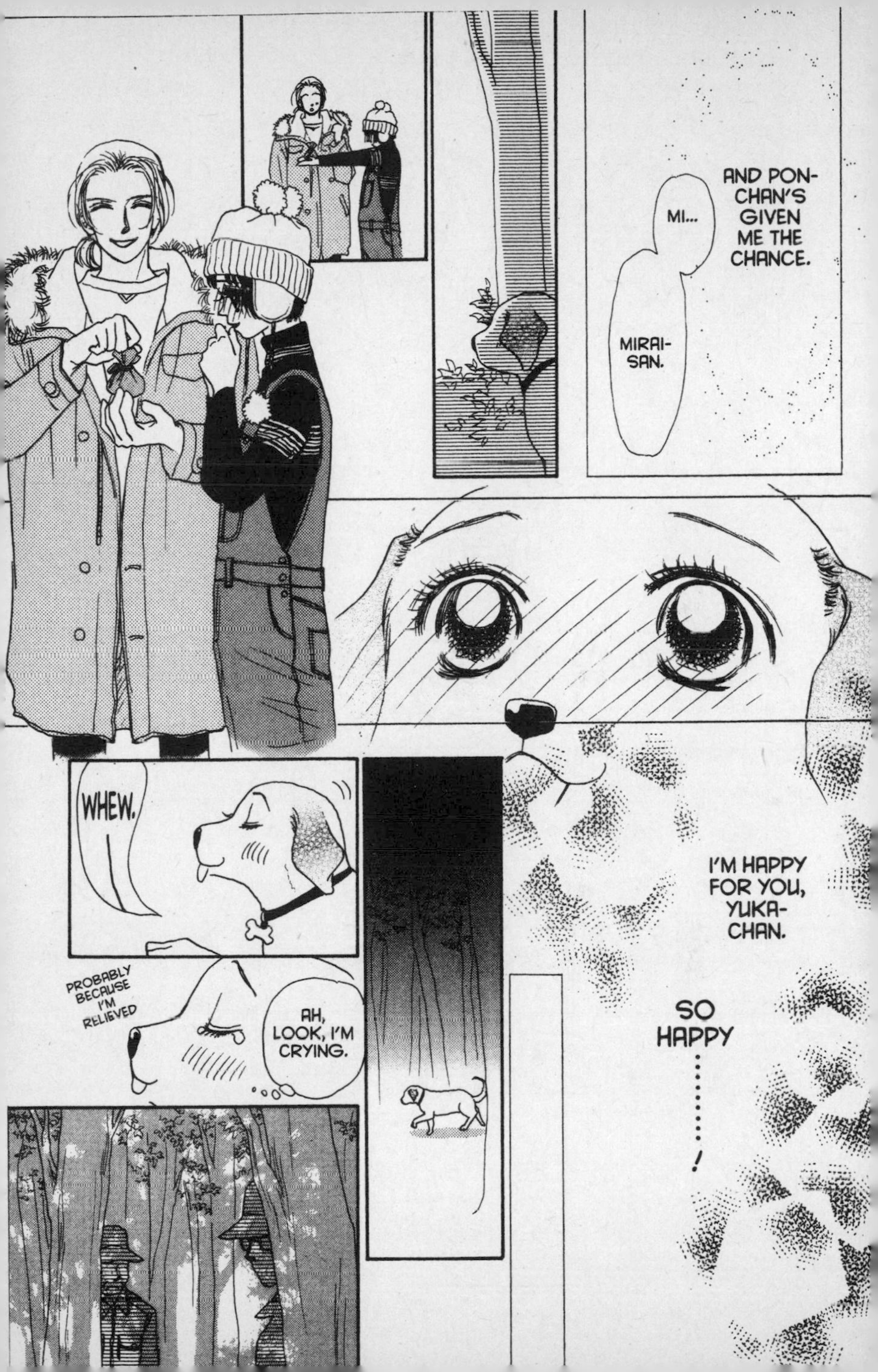
AND PON-CHAN'S GIVEN ME THE CHANCE.
MI...
MIRAI-SAN.
I'M HAPPY FOR YOU, YUKA-CHAN.
SO HAPPY ......!
WHEW.
AH, LOOK, I'M CRYING.
PROBABLY BECAUSE I'M RELIEVED

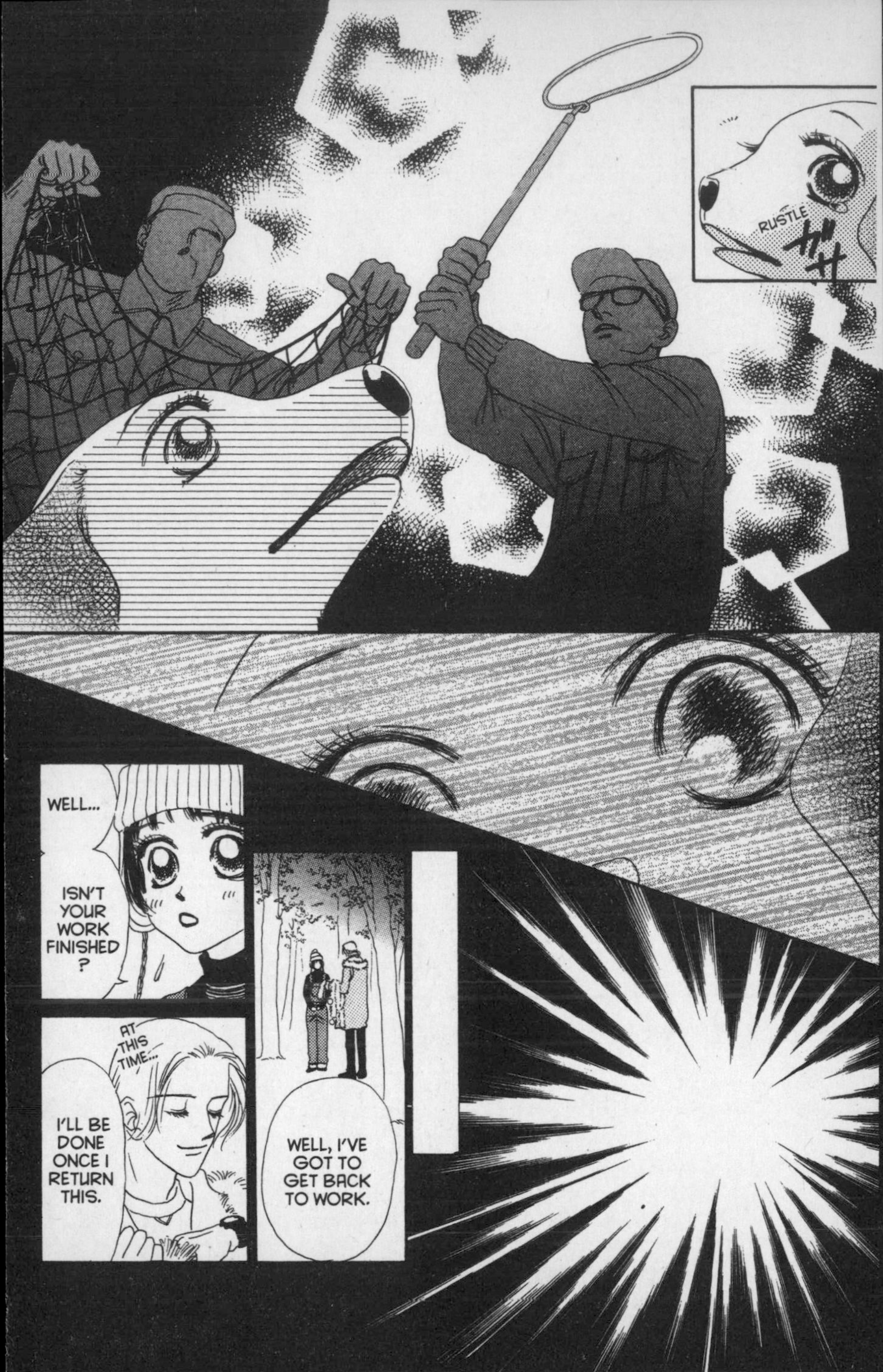
RUSTLE
WELL...
ISN'T YOUR WORK FINISHED?
AT THIS TIME...
I'LL BE DONE ONCE I RETURN THIS.
WELL, I'VE GOT TO GET BACK TO WORK.

THEN, WILL YOU COME TO MY HOUSE AFTER YOU'RE DONE?
PON-CHAN WILL BE THERE AS WELL.
PON-CHAN, TOO?
......
OH!
MIRAI-KUN, YOU'VE COME AT A GOOD TIME!
ISN'T THIS A SPECTACULAR TREE?!
OH YEAH!
UH...
WHERE IS IT?
I CAN'T BELIEVE IT'S RIGHT AT OUR FEET...
AH HA HA
IT WAS TOO HUGE SO I COULDN'T SET IT UP.

AH, I'M SORRY TO TROUBLE YOU, MIRAI-KUN.
HE WAS ASKED TO PLANT IT.
I'M USED TO IT.
CRUNCH
CRUNCH
S-SORRY MIRAI-SAN.
IT'S OKAY, IT'S OKAY.
WHAT'S THIS?
CLACK
A ROCK PERHAPS?
HEH HEH, PONTA WENT TO ALL THIS TROUBLE TO HIDE THIS PRESENT SHE GOT FROM SOMEBODY.
YUKA-CHAN?

I HOPE MIRAI-KUN WILL BE HAPPY WITH THIS PRESENT.
WAIT HERE.
PON-CHAN......!
OJI-CHAMA, WHERE'S PON-CHAN?!
UH...
SHE'S NOT WITH YOU?
BARK
BARK
BARK

WHERE AM I? LET ME OUT!
BARK
BARK
BARK
BARK
COME ON!
SHUT UP, NEWBIE!
BARK
BARK
YOU'RE NOT GOING TO GET OUT OF HERE BY CAUSING A RUCKUS!
PON-CHAAAN!
PON-CHAAAN!
PON-CHAAAN!
PON-CHAAAN!
...
WHY'S EVERYONE SO GLUM?
CHEER UP!
TODAY'S CHRISTMAS!
CHRISTMAS?
YEP!!
IN THE HUMAN WORLD, TODAY'S THE DAY TO EAT FOOD AND GIVE PRESENTS.
F-FOOD?!
HAH, DON'T BE STUPID.

WE DON'T WANT TO HEAR ABOUT THE PEOPLE WHO ABANDONED US!
LUNK
ぬっ
THAT'S RIGHT! THAT'S RIGHT!
MY OWNER WAS A GOOD PERSON.
UNEASY
HMPH, IDIOT.
EVEN THOUGH YOU WERE ABANDONED.
WH... WHAT?
IT DOESN'T MATTER.
SNIFF SNIFF
WE'RE NEVER GOING TO SEE OUR OLD OWNERS AGAIN ANYWAY.
CHIHUAHUA
HUH?
NEVER SEE THEM AGAIN?
LABRADORS HAVE NO WORRIES BECAUSE THEY'RE SO POPULAR.
I WAS ABANDONED BECAUSE I'M OUT OF STYLE.
YOU'LL FIND A NEW OWNER IN NO TIME.
NEW OWNER ....?
NEVER SEE THEM...
AGAIN?

THAT'S IT, THAT'S IT, GOOD GIRL.
WHAT IS IT, PONTA?
COME HERE, PON-CHAN!
ポトポトッ
DRIP DRIP

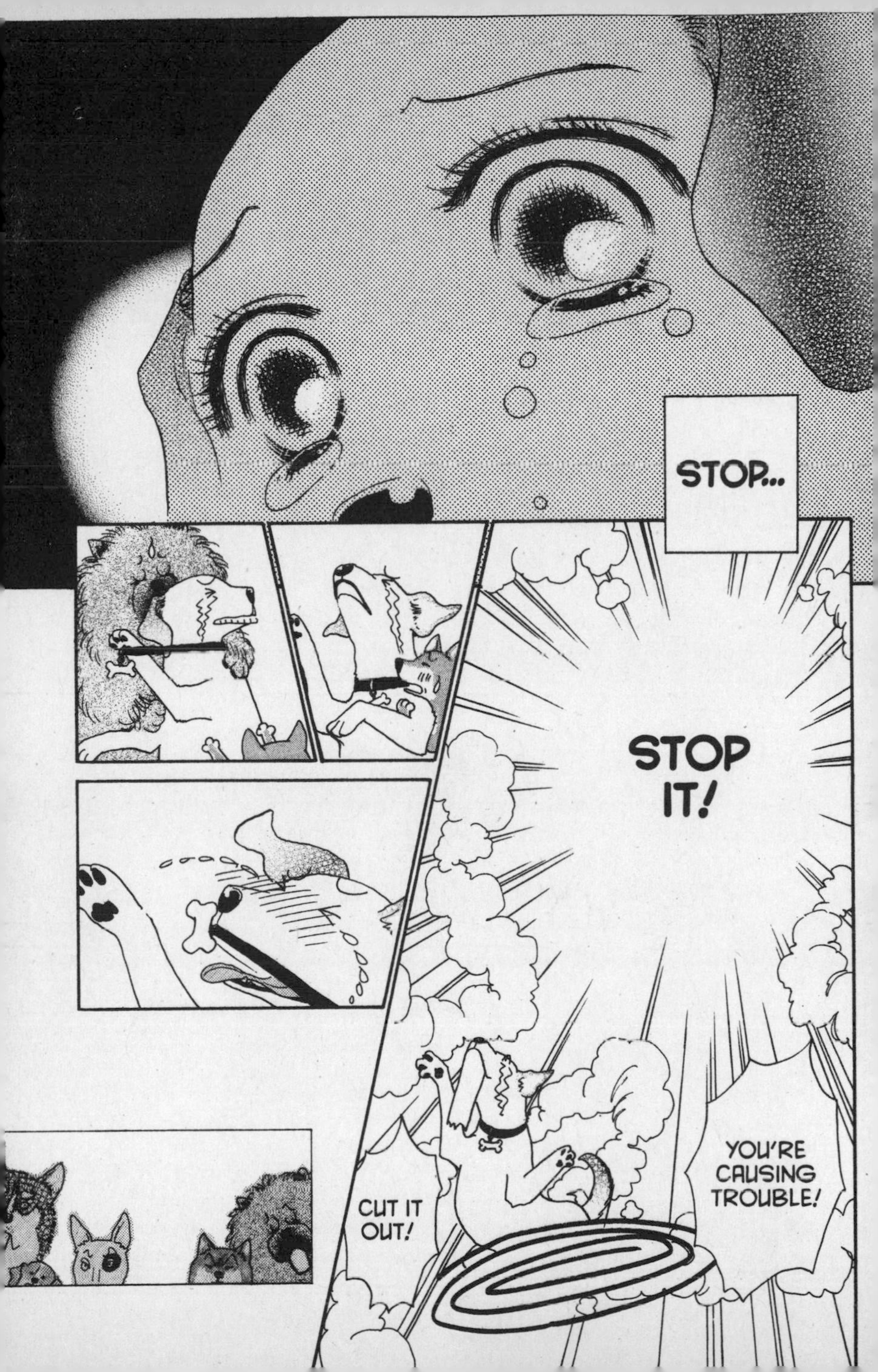
STOP...
STOP IT!
YOU'RE CAUSING TROUBLE!
CUT IT OUT!

YELP
YELP
WOOF
WOOF
IF YOU'RE LOOKING FOR A YELLOW LAB, SHE'S RIGHT OVER HERE.
WOOF
YELP
YELP
YELP
YELP
WOOF
WOOF
WOOF
WOOF
WOOF

W-WHAT THE?
PON-CHAN!

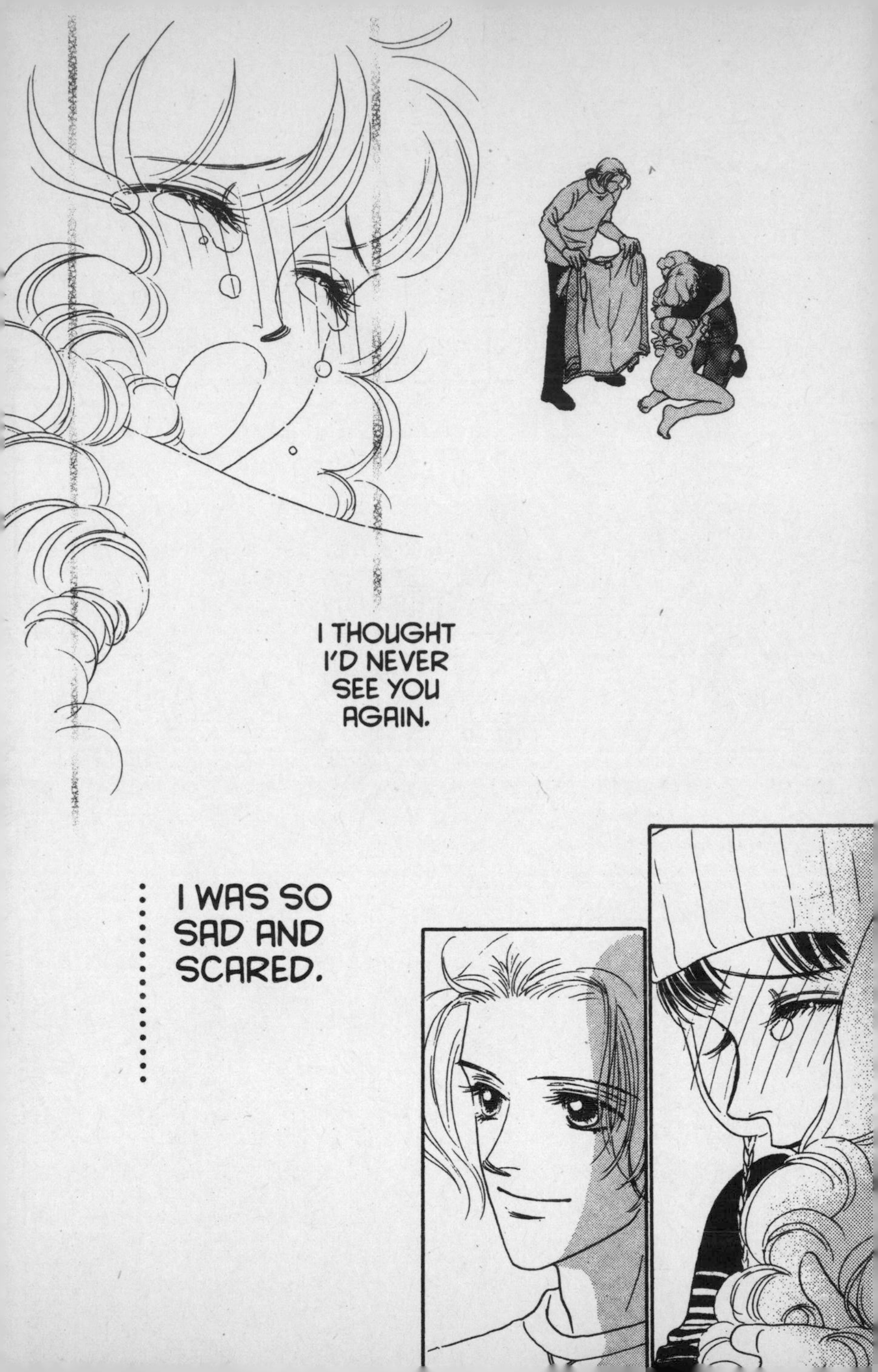
I THOUGHT I'D NEVER SEE YOU AGAIN.
...... I WAS SO SAD AND SCARED.

I'M HUMAN
IN FRONT OF MIRAI-KUN AND YUKA-CHAN!
IT'S OKAY PON-CHAN!
WHETHER YOU'RE A DOG OR HUMAN...
THE ONLY THING THAT MATTERS IS THAT YOU'RE WITH US, PON-CHAN.
I'M SORRY...
FOR CAUSING YOU SO MUCH PAIN.
I'M SORRY, PON-CHAN.
......

THEY'RE NOT COLD?
HO HO, YUKA'S SO SILLY
WELL THEY SAID THEY WANTED TO HAVE CHRISTMAS, JUST THE THREE OF THEM.
MERRY CHRISTMAS!
I'LL TRY IT ON.
WOW, THIS IS GREAT.
THANKS YUKA-CHAN.
WHISPER WHISPER
HEY, YOU TOO, PON-CHAN.
Y-YEAH.

HERE YOU GO, MIRAI-KUN!!
HEH HEH.
わくわく THRILL THRILL
にこにこ GRIN GRIN
わくわく THRILL THRILL
SO THAT'S WHAT THIS WAS?
AH...
THANK YOU, PONTA.
I'M REALLY HAPPY.
IT'S THE THOUGHT THAT COUNTS.
WELL, IT'S NOT REALLY A PRESENT BUT...
I'VE GOT SOMETHING FOR YOU, TOO.
YIPPEE!
YIPPEE! YAY!

AAH
SOME-THING FOR PON-CHAN. LUCKY DEVIL.
NO, NO. SOMETHING ALL THREE OF US CAN HAVE FUN WITH.
A BALL!
WHAH ♡
PONTA!
SPRING
MERRY CHRISTMAS!!
END OF CHAPTER 5

CHAPTER
NUMBER
6
THE GUY WHO CAUSES A STORM

ぷく
PUFF
ぷくううう
PUFF
HA HA, PON-CHAN.
STOP IMITATING THE MOCHI AND COME HERE.

OKAY THEN.
HAPPY NEW YEAR ~!!
PONT'S PORTION
HAPPY NEW YEAR ~♡
WHAT? I DON'T KNOW WHAT THIS IS ALL ABOUT BUT...
THIS LOOKS DELICIOUS.
CHOMP
んが
WHIZZ
GOO
にちゃあ
STRETCH
びょーん

GRIN
SOME-THING TO DRINK?
WHAT'S THIS?
SNIFF SNIFF
AH!
STING
HEE HEE
IT'S HIT YOUR NOSE.
SNORT WHEEZE
OJI-CHAMA, I CAN'T BELIEVE YOU'RE GIVING PON-CHAN O-TOSO.
BUTTERFLIES
THAT SPICED SAKE'S GOOD, REAL GOOD.
FOR A LONG LIFE
LICK
YOU DRANK IT, YOU DRANK IT!
WITH THAT, YOU'LL LIVE A LONG LIFE.
GULP
AAH.
WHIZZ
MORE.
AAAH.

WHA HA HA.
HEH HEH
WE'RE THE KASHIMASHI MUSUME.
IWAKI
© GEORGE ASAKURA♥♥♥
ぱっぱっぱっ
WNG WNG WNG
D-DON'T CREEP UP ON ME LIKE THAT!
HEY
S-SORRY.
WHAT ?!
YOU SPOKE ?!

WHOA! I THOUGHT PONTA SPOKE FOR A SECOND.
S-SORRY ABOUT THAT.
HE WAS REALLY SUCKERED IN BY PON-CHAN.
WELL, COME NOW, IT'S OKAY. DRINK UP.
OLD MAN →
どんッ
THUD
I'VE GOT THE FEELING THEY'RE PLAYING A TRICK ON ME BUT...
OKAY, THANK YOU.
とくとくとくとく
GLUG GLUG GLUG
ぷはーッ
AAAH
THAT DOES THE TRICK
ブルルッ
QUIVER
ふ〜ら
WOBBLE
ふ〜〜ら〜
WOBBLE
PONTA?
CLONK
カチャカチャ
RATTLE RATTLE
......

YOU CAN'T OPEN IT, HUH? OKAY, I'M COMING.
BY ANY CHANCE... IS SHE DRUNK?
VERY.
COME SIT UNDER THE KOTATSU.
O-OKAY.
T-THE TWO OF US ALONE...
WHAT...
WHAT SHOULD I SAY...?
PON-CHAAN!
I-I'M GOING TO LOOK FOR PON-CHAN.
JOLT

PON-CHAN.
PON-CHAN.
AH.
STEAM STEAM
ホヤホヤ…
……
SHE DID HER BUSINESS THERE
..AH.
HUH?
PO...
PANT PANT PANT
ハッハッハッ
WHEEZE WHEEZE WHEEZE
ハッハッ
PON-CHAN ……

YOU'VE TURNED YOURSELF INTO A SNOWMAN.
THAT'S TOO FUNNY
YUKA! I'M GOING OUT FOR A WHILE.
OH, THAT'S RIGHT. WE'RE VISITING RELATIVES.
SORRY PONTA. YOU'RE STAYING HOME.
THE PEOPLE WE'RE SEEING DON'T LIKE DOGS
NO, NO, I WANT TO GO TOO
UM...
I COULD WATCH PONTA.
I'VE GOT NOTHING BETTER TO DO ANYWAY
UH, WELL...
WAG WAG WAG
SHE SEEMS PRETTY HAPPY WITH THAT.
SO DO YOU.
WELL, BUT...
PREMIUM CHOICE
KIKUMASAMUNE

HOW DOES THIS TURN YOU FROM A DOG TO A HUMAN?
HUH
KISS
んちゅっ
JUST AS I THOUGHT. IT DOESN'T WORK FOR ME.
HE REALLY WANTED TO TRY BEING A DOG
HA HA HA
BUT WHEN YOU DO IT...
SMOOTCH
SHAZAM
ボワーン
I'M HUMAN ~~!
AND THEN?
IN THE BLINK OF AN EYE...
CACKLE CACKLE
ケラケラ
WHAH
はっ
......

WHAT'RE YOU DOING?! THROW THIS ON!
...PUT IT ON.
WHAT?! I DON'T NEED THAT.
WEAR IT!
WHY? WHY?
HUMAN'S NORMALLY WEAR CLOTHES. IT'S EMBARRASSING TO BE NAKED.
...HMM
HEY, HEY!
MIRAI-KUN!
YOU PUT IT ON
WHAT?
WHOOSH
ARE YOU TEASING ME?
WELL, I DON'T KNOW WHAT 'EMBARRASSING' MEANS.
NEVER MIND THAT. PUT IT ON, I'M...
YOU'RE WHAT?

YOU'RE GETTING ME IN THE MOOD.
FOR WHAT ?

COME ON, WHAT? I WANT TO DO IT, TOO.
I WANNA DO IT!
I WANNA DO IT!
I WANNA DO IT!
NEVER MIND.
KEEP IT DOWN. BE QUIET.
WITH THINGS AS THEY ARE, IF WE DID THAT I'D BE...
'THE PERVERT WHO DOES IT WITH DOGS'.
DAZE
IT'S GOT TO BE THE BOOZE TALKING.
SNUGGLE
EH HEH HEH
I FEEL SO AT EASE WHEN I DO THIS.
I CAN FEEL YOUR WARMTH.
HOW ABOUT YOU, MIRAI-KUN?

UM...
JUST AS I ALREADY KNEW...
I LOVE MIRAI-KUN
......
YEAH.
IT FEELS PRETTY GOOD TO ME, TOO.
CHUCKLE
HEH HEH.
I'M GLAD.
A LOVE WITH HER CAN NEVER BE.
......
...MIRAI-KUN.
......
WHAT?

WAKE UP.
WAKE UP, MIRAI-KUN.
RUB
....
WHOO HOO! YOU'RE AWAKE ~♡

PO-
PONTA?
JI-CHAN AND YUKA-CHAN BOTH COMPLIMENTED ME
AM I CUTE? AM I CUTE?
BED HEAD
A-AHH,
EVEN THE DOG'S DRESSED UP.
GRIN
LET'S GO TO THIS HATSUMODE THING.
IT SOUNDS DELICIOUS
ARE YOU TIRED?
NO.
UP UNTIL NOW, I WAS OUT COLD FROM DRINKING LAST NIGHT.
GOOD MORNING.
I DON'T KNOW WHEN PONTA WENT HOME.
HUNG-OVER
DON'T RUSH AHEAD OF US, PON-CHAN.
COMPARED TO THEM SHE'S...
ZOOM

HEY
IT'S HARD TO RUN IN THIS.
SO ENERGETIC, SHE'S RUINING HER KIMONO.
WHOA!
SO MANY PEOPLE!
どおおおー
TWIRL
YEAH!
STOP PLAYING AROUND.

HOLD MY HAND.
P-PON-CHAN, YOU GO IN THE MIDDLE.
BLUSH
HOW AWKWARD
AHHHH!
THUMP
THUMP
THUMP
OH, TOO BAD.
SILLY.

FLICK
PON-CHAN?!
DASH
YOU FOOL! DON'T CHASE IT!
I-LOST SIGHT OF HER ...
KYA! WHAT THE?!
I STEPPED ON SOMETHING.
OUCH.
I'VE HAD IT WITH THIS.
STRETCH
PON-CHAN!
COME BACK, PONTA!
AH...

SPRING
KYA!
A DOG!
THIS IS MORE LIKE A CAT ♪
SCAMPER
SCAMPER
MORE AND MORE CAT-LIKE. NO, MORE SPECTACULAR THAN A CAT!
TAP
TAP
TAP

SPRING
I'VE GOT IT!
AAH
LET ME THROUGH.
I DID IT
I'M GOOD
UH?

KYAAAAAAAAA!
PONTA!
THUD

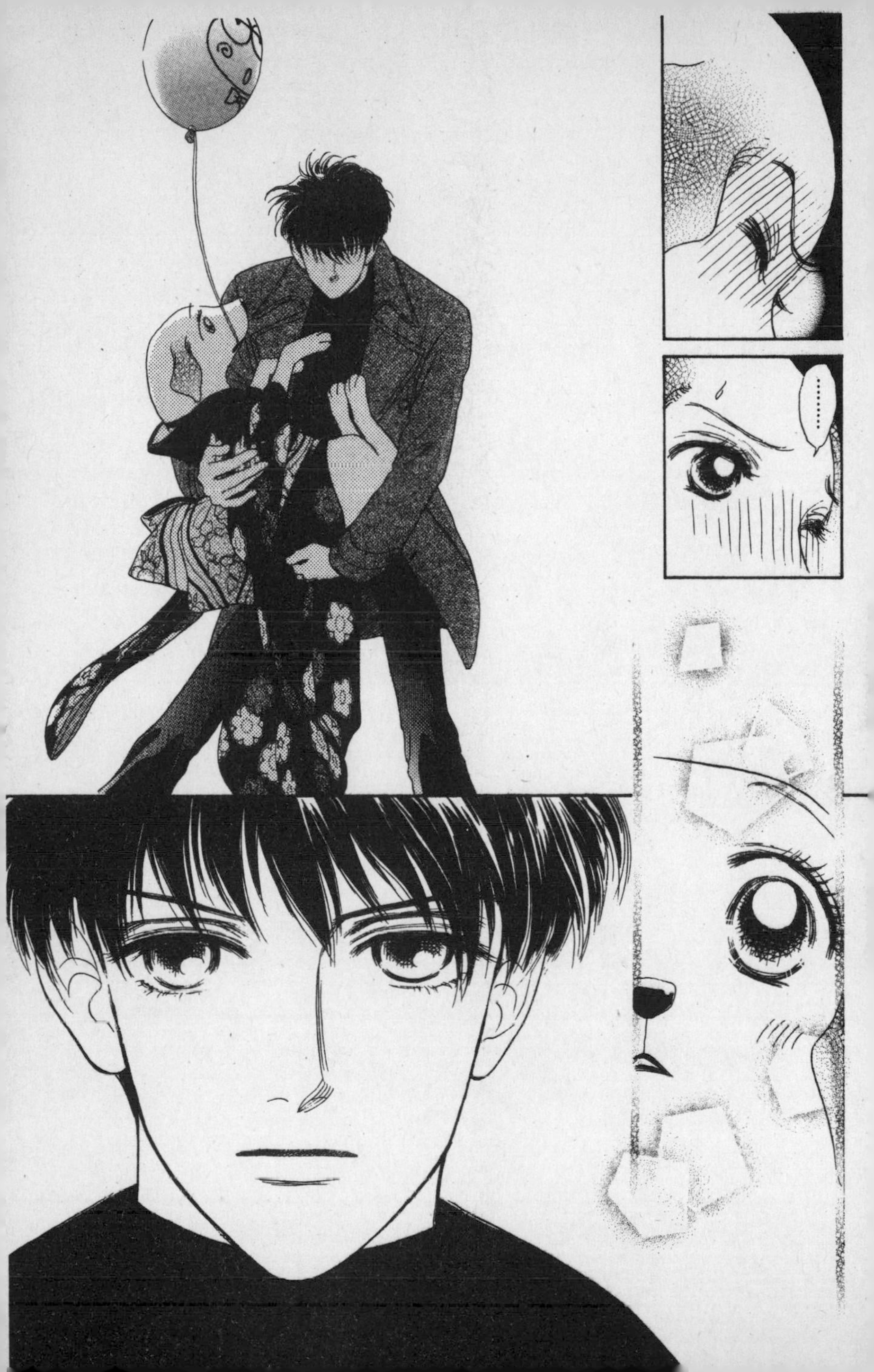

THAT WAS FOOLISH OF YOU, ACTING SO RECKLESS. DOGS DON'T ALWAYS LAND ON THEIR FEET.
T-THANK YOU SO MUCH.
BE CAREFUL, FOOLISH PARENT.
BALLOON BALLOON
FOOLISH PARENT
PONTA!
THANK YOU. SHE'S WITH US.
CRACK

KYAH...
THUD
KYA!
MIRAI-KUN!
DOG'S AREN'T TOYS FOR HUMANS!!

DON'T MAKE A DOG WEAR A KIMONO AND PARADE IT AROUND IN A CROWD!
AND WITH A GIRL IN TOW TO BOOT!
STOP SCREWING AROUND!
I HATE FLASHY GUYS LIKE YOU!

HE SAVED ME SO I THINK HE'S A GOOD PERSON BUT...
I WON'T STAND FOR ANY CRUELTY TOWARDS MIRAI-KUN!
....
YOU'RE GOING TO PROTECT THAT KIND OF OWNER?
THAT'S SAD.
BECAUSE YOU HAVE SUCH INNOCENT LOOKING EYES, I'LL FORGIVE YOU TODAY.
THINK ABOUT WHAT YOU DID, SCUMBAG.
AN ANIMAL'S HEART IS A BEAUTIFUL THING.
COMPARED TO A HUMAN'S...
SIGH...

WHAT'S THE USE......
WHOOSH
ゴオ
IS THAT GUY A RONIN?
あぜん......
DUMBSTRUCK
OUCH.
AH!
MIRAI-KUN LOOKS LIKE HE'S IN PAIN.
LICK
ぺろ...
THANK YOU, PONTA.
BUT I'M FINE SO WHY DON'T YOU TRANSFORM BACK.
SOME-WHERE OUT OF SIGHT
AH, HE'S RIGHT. YOU CAN'T RIDE THE TRAIN LIKE THAT.
GOSH
THAT GETUP'S WEIRD

SORRY, MIRAI-KUN.
NOW THAT I THINK ABOUT IT.
IT WAS MY FAULT.
OH YEAH, IT WAS YOUR FAULT ALL RIGHT.
IT'S NOT HARD TO FIGURE THAT OUT.
CRESTFALLEN
WELL, I'LL FORGIVE YOU.
HEH HEH
YOU PROTECTED ME BACK THERE AND ALL
WELL, THAT GUY WAS AWFUL.
I KNOW THAT MUCH.
BUT THE TRUTH IS, I STOPPED HIM.
Y-YOU'RE RIGHT.
I GOT IT...
IF I COME ACROSS HIM AGAIN, I'LL APOLOGIZE.
DON'T SAY SUCH AN OMINOUS THING.
WE'RE NOT GOING TO SEE HIM AGAIN.
WHY NOT?
HE'LL HIT ME AGAIN.
IF HE TRIES, I'LL BITE HIM BEFORE HE CAN DO THAT.
CHOMP!
......
YOU'RE S-SCARY, PON-CHAN

IF I BECOME A TRANSFER STUDENT.
A TRANSFER STUDENT.
PERHAPS I CAN MAKE...
A HUNDRED FRIENDS.

THIS IS FUJINAGA GO-KUN.
BECAUSE OF HIS FATHER'S WORK, HE'S LIVING IN TOKYO NOW.
NO WAY
NO WAY
ISN'T HE GALLANT?
YEAH. HE'S HANDSOME.
WELL THEN, PLEASE INTRODUCE YOURSELF.
OHH.
I'M DEAD MEAT

FUJINAGA
?
ANGER MARK
HE'LL HIT ME AGAIN
IF HE TRIES, I'LL...
CLATTER
CHOMP
KOIZUMI
?!
RIP

I WANT TO APOLOGIZE FOR THE OTHER DAY.
LOOK HERE!
WHOA!
IF YOU KEEP SAYING STUPID STUFF, YOU'LL GIVE YOUR IDENTITY AWAY.
DON'T MIND HER.
BLUBBER BLUBBER
HA HA HA
WHISPER WHISPER
B-BUT...
THAT GIRL...
..LIKES THAT GUY?

THAT JERKY SHOWOFF!
HE BROUGHT ANOTHER GIRL TO THE HATSUMODE THOUGH.
UH, FUJINAGA-KUN, YOUR SEAT IS NEAR THE HALLWAY...
U-UH?
FUJINAGA?
THUD
TOSS
W-WHAT'RE YOU DOING?

HEY, HEY. WE'LL SEE JI-CHAN AT THE OPENING CEREMONY, RIGHT?
OH, PROB-ABLY.
THAT TRANSFER STUDENT DOESN'T LISTEN AT ALL.
YEAH, HE'S SCARY.
YEAH, YEAH
YAY! THAT'LL BE FUN!

YOU...
SHOULD GIVE UP ON THAT GUY.
AND CHOOSE ME.
END OF CHAPTER 6

PON-CHAN THE GUY MAGNET?

PUFF

GIVE UP ON THAT GUY.
CHOOSE ME.
STARE
キョトン
'CHOOSE ME'...
MEANS WHAT?
WHAT DO YOU WANT TO DO WITH ME?
UH?!
ぴと
SNUGGLE

BLUSH
......AH.
WHOA.
MIRAI-KUN, MIRAI-KUN.
THIS IS THE FIRST TIME I'VE SEEN SOMEONE SO RED.
I TOLD YOU TO CUT IT OUT.
A- ANYWAY...
GIVE UP ON THAT GUY.
HE'S NOT A DECENT GUY!!
THAT'S ALL I HAVE TO SAY. SEE YA!!
THAT'S STRANGE.
HE TOOK OFF.
WHAT'S THIS?

SELF-INTRODUCTION.
CIAO! I'M GO FUJINAGA.
BIG SMILE
THE CHARACTER FOR 'GO' IS THE SAME AS THE KINKI KID'S TSUYOSHI. AT FIRST GLANCE, PEOPLE SAY I LOOK SCARY BUT INSIDE, I'M SO CHEERFUL! NICE TO MEET YOU!!
WAVE AT THIS TIME
......
I'LL PRETEND I NEVER SAW THAT.
CREEPY
? ?
I CAN'T READ THIS
GSSSH
SPLASH
SPLASH
SPLASH
HAH
HAH
HAH
HAH
THE FIRST TIME I MEET THE GIRL I SAY, 'CHOOSE ME'. WHAT HAVE I DONE?!
うあああああ
AAAH.
AND ON TOP OF THAT...

THE INSTANT I SAW THAT GUY'S FACE, I BLEW THE SELF-INTRODUCTION I SPENT ALL NIGHT WRITING.
SLUMP
THIS TIME WHEN I TRANSFERRED, I WAS GOING TO TAKE THE OPPORTUNITY TO MAKE A LOT OF FRIENDS.
MY H-HANDKERCHIEF ...
JUST CALM DOWN
FIDDLE
THAT'S RIGHT. YOU'VE ONLY JUST STARTED HERE.
WHERE'S MY SPEECH ....?
SELF-INTRODUCTION.
CIAO! I'M GO FUJINAGA.
BIG SMILE
THE CHARACTER FOR 'GO' IS THE SAME AS THE KINKI KID'S TSUYOSHI. AT FIRST GLANCE, PEOPLE SAY I LOOK SCARY BUT INSIDE, I'M SO CHEERFUL!
NICE TO MEET YOU!!
WAVE AT THIS TIME
HERE.
YOU DROPPED IT.

MIRAI-KUN! MIRAI-KUN!
THIS GUY'S BLUE THIS TIME!
DID YOU L-LOOK AT IT?
DREAD
YEAH, I LOOKED AT IT.
THE ONLY THING SHE DID WAS LOOK AT IT.
CIAO! FUJI. KINKI KID'S TSUYOSHI. SO CHEERFUL.
YOU... DIDN'T LAUGH?
WHY WOULD I LAUGH?
BLUSH

じーーん
MOVED
THIS GIRL'S TERRIFIC.
MIRAI-KUN!
IT'S AMAZING!
NOW HIS CHEEK'S TURNED PINK!
W-WAIT.
I DIDN'T MEAN ANYTHING BAD. I REALLY JUST WANTED YOU TO STOP HANGING AROUND THAT GUY.
HE'S A TERRIBLE GUY WHO'S TRICKING YOU.
WHAT DO YOU MEAN, TRICK?
I MEAN, EVEN THOUGH HE PUTS ON A GOOD ACT WHEN HE'S WITH YOU, YOU DON'T KNOW WHAT HE'S DOING WHEN YOU'RE NOT AROUND.
IN FACT, I'VE SEEN HIM
IT'S HARD FOR ME TO TELL YOU BUT...
I SAW HIM WITH ANOTHER GIRL AT THE HATSUMODE AND ON TOP OF THAT, HE ABUSED AN ANIMAL.
HMM?
BUT I LOVE MIRAI-KUN!

MIRAI-KUN!
とててて
SCAMPER SCAMPER
I CAN'T BELIEVE SHE'S SO OBSESSED!
I CAN'T BELIEVE IT...
A HEART THAT'S PURE AND TRUE.
PONTA?!
THERE'S QUITE A STRONG BREEZE TODAY.
AND THOSE CRYSTAL CLEAR EYES, IT'S AS IF THEY'RE REFLECTING THAT HEART.
ドキン
THUMP
ドキン
THUMP
ドキン
THUMP
I CAN'T BELIEVE SUCH A GIRL EXISTS IN THIS WORLD.
ぱあぁ…
BURST
MY DREAM ...!!!
SPRING'S IN FULL BLOOM IN HIS HEAD ONLY.

MY DREAM GIRL!
KOIZUMI-SAN!
THIS ISN'T TAG!
DASH
KOIZUMI-SAN!
SMASH
STRIKE! YOU'RE OUT!
......
CHOMP
MUNCH
GLUG
GLUG GLUG
SHE'S ALWAYS LIVING IN THE MOMENT...
SHE'S SO DIFFERENT FROM GIRLS WHO ARE ONLY BEAUTIFUL ON THE OUTSIDE.
SNOOZE
ZZZZZ
SNOOZE
BLUSH
AH!
SNOOZE
ZZZZZ
SNOOZE

WHACK
AAARGH
WHACK
WHACK
WHAT IN THE WORLD AM I DOING?!
WHAT'S THAT ABOUT?
KYA HA HA
BUT I CAN'T GET HER OUT OF MY MIND!
THIS IS HOW HE SEES HER.
I...
WHEN I LOOK AT THAT GIRL, I FEEL I CAN DO ANYTHING.
151
LAB ROOM
FUJINAGA?
FUJINAGA JUST TRANSFERRED AND ALREADY HE'S SKIPPING CLASS?

251
HOME ECONOMICS
OKAY, TOMORROW'S VALENTINE'S DAY SO LET'S MAKE SOME TRUFFLES.
VALENTINES DAY ISN'T VERY EXCITING THIS YEAR IS IT?
CHATTER
YOU CAN SAY THAT AGAIN. I'D RATHER RECEIVE THAN GIVE.
HEY, OVER HERE!
WHAT'S VALENTINE'S DAY?
SAY WHAT?!
YOU DON'T KNOW ABOUT VALENTINE'S DAY?!
NO WAY! THAT'S SO WEIRD!
EVERYONE, THAT'S RUDE.
PONTA-SAN'S A RETURNEE SO IT'S ONLY NATURAL THAT SHE DOESN'T KNOW ABOUT IT.
IS THAT RIGHT?
SLAM
YEAH BUT
THAT'S RIGHT, IT'S RUDE!

WHO'S THAT AGAIN?
BEATS ME.
...
CLASS-REP KNOWS, RIGHT?
FLINCH
HUH ?!
T-THIS IS BAD. I DON'T REMEMBER WHO THIS IS AND AS CLASS-REP, I'LL LOSE FACE.
HEY, SO WHAT'S VALENTINE'S DAY ~~?
AH
I-I'LL EXPLAIN!
LET ME CUT TO THE POINT.
VALENTINE'S DAY IS A HOLIDAY ON FEBRUARY 14 THAT COMMEMORATES SAINT VALENTINE, A ROMAN DISCIPLE OF THE MARTYRED CHRIST THAT LIVED AROUND THE THIRD CENTURY. ON THIS DAY, GIRLS GIVE PRESENTS AND CARDS TO GUYS WHO THEY'VE TAKEN A FANCY TO.
EXCERPT FROM THE NIHONGO DAIJITEN (KODANSHA)
SCRATCH
SCRATCH
WHAT PART OF THAT WAS 'TO THE POINT'?
LOOKS LIKE LICE
IN SHORT, IT'S A DAY GIRLS TELL BOYS THEY LIKE THEM.
ALONG WITH CHOCOLATES.
I'LL DO IT!
I WANT TO DO THAT ~~~!

NOW THAT I THINK ABOUT IT...
I HAVEN'T TOLD MIRAI-KUN IN WORDS, 'I LOVE YOU'.
COME AND GET YOUR INGREDIENTS.
I'M COMING ~~~!
EACH GROUPS' INGREDIENTS ARE HERE.
NOW, I'LL EXPLAIN THE PROCEDURE.
SENSEI, KOIZUMI-SAN'S...
CHOCOLATE'S...
SO DELICIOUS ~~~!
PLEASE WATCH OVER HER, CLASS-REP.
IT MIGHT BE TOUGH BUT...
LEAVE IT TO ME.
CAN I JOIN TOO?
SHE'S STILL EATING
TAKING MEASURES TO ISOLATE PONTA
GLARE
ぬっ
OH, OF COURSE.
SOMEHOW ...
I'VE GOT A BAD FEELING ABOUT THIS.

COMMOTION
わい わい
GOOD JOB.
CHATTER CHATTER
ざわ ざわ
KYA
THIS GROUP ALSO DID WELL.
COMMOTION
わい わい
UGH.
ぐちゃ
SHAMBLES
LOOKS DELICIOUS, HUH?
EXPERIENCING THE FIRST FAILURE IN A CLASS SINCE BIRTH.
WHAT ABOUT THE CHOCOLATES ~~~?
NO THANKS.
YOU TWO CAN DIVVY THEM UP.
I (DEEP VOICE), I MEAN...
I'M OKAY (HIGH VOICE). YOU CAN HAVE THEM.
REALLY?! ALL OF THEM?!

WHAHOO
MIRAI-KUN WILL BE SO HAPPY.
STUN
OF COURSE
IT'S NO SURPRISE SHE'S GOING TO GIVE THEM TO HIM!
OH, HEY.
YOU'RE NOT GOING TO GIVE THEM TO THAT TRANSFER STUDENT?!
WHAT'S HIS NAME, GO-KUN?
MAYBE I'LL GIVE MINE TO HIM?
HMM?
YOU'RE GOING TO GIVE YOURSELF CHOCOLATES?
THAT'S WEIRD.
IS SHE ON TO ME?
EVEN THOUGH NO ONE ELSE DID, SHE KNEW.
SHE KNEW......!!

I'M A VALENTINE.
I'M A VALENTINE.
I HOPE MIRAI-KUN LIKES THESE CHOCOLATES.
I HOPE HE TELLS ME THEY'RE DELICIOUS.
...
SMELLS GOOD.
DROOL.
NO. NO.
SQUIRM
THEY'RE FOR MIRAI-KUN TO EAT.
......
MUNCH...
はむ...
J- JUST ONE.
JUST ONE PIECE.
DELICIOUS!
AAAH.
THAT HIT THE SPOT.
AND NOW...
I'LL REALLY GET SOME SLEEP.
......
DROOL.

GRIN
にかー
HERE YOU ARE, MIRAI-KUN!!
ROLLL...

WHAT'S THIS?
AT FIRST GLANCE, IT LOOKS LIKE A PIECE OF POO.
IT LOOKS DELICIOUS, RIGHT?
THEY DIDN'T LAST LONG THOUGH.
I MADE IT YESTERDAY IN HOME ECONOMICS.
COULD IT BE THAT, THIS...
IS IT REALLY 'CHOCOLATE' ~~~~~?
IS CHOCOLATE?
PIN PON PIN PON!
VALENTINE'S DAY!
YAY
I...
LIKE YOU, MIRAI-KUN!

DO YOU LIKE ME, MIRAI-KUN?
DO YOU LIKE ME, MIRAI-KUN?
DO YOU LIKE ME?
クス
CHUCKLE
I LIKE YOU.
MIRAI-KUN, I
LO
VE
YOU!
DO YOU LOVE ME?!
HMM, THAT'S A BIG STEP.
I'M NOT SURE I CAN SAY LOVE ......
TEE HEE.
I'M KIDDING, KIDDING. I LOVE YOU.
REALLY?!

I'M SO HAPPY! I'M SO HAPPY!
WHA HOO!
I'M SO HAPPY!
EASY THERE.
OH HO HO
YOU'RE A SIMPLE MINDED ONE, YOU.
HA HA HA
PLEASE HAVE A CHOCOLATE.
OH, THANK YOU.
THIS TREE, WHAT KIND OF TREE IS IT? I'M CON-CERNED ABOUT THIS TREE.
HEE HEE.

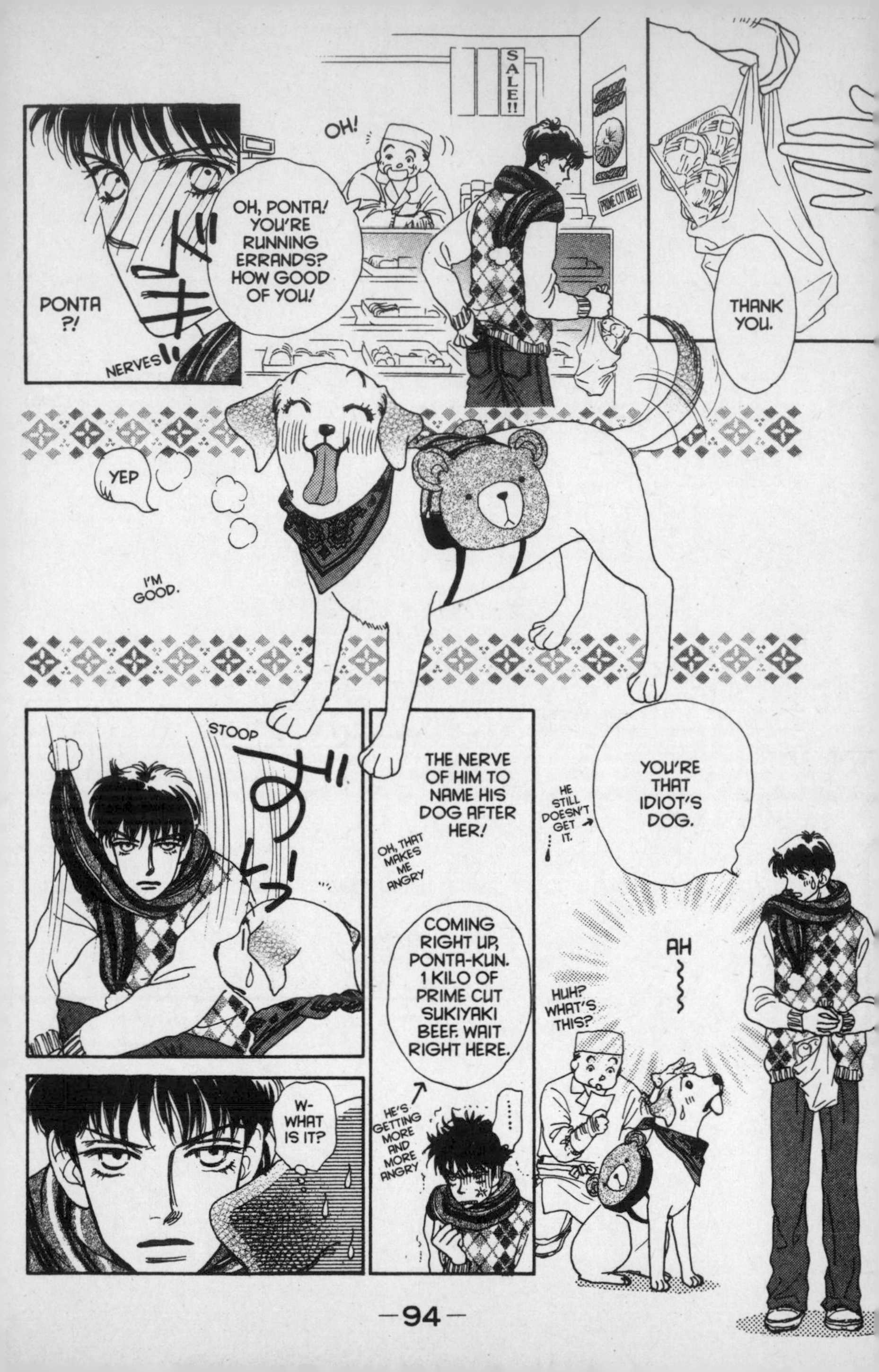
SALE!!
PRIME CUT BEEF
OH!
OH, PONTA! YOU'RE RUNNING ERRANDS? HOW GOOD OF YOU!
PONTA ?!
NERVES
THANK YOU.
YEP
I'M GOOD.
YOU'RE THAT IDIOT'S DOG.
HE STILL DOESN'T GET IT.
THE NERVE OF HIM TO NAME HIS DOG AFTER HER!
OH, THAT MAKES ME ANGRY
STOOP
AH
HUH? WHAT'S THIS?
COMING RIGHT UP, PONTA-KUN. 1 KILO OF PRIME CUT SUKIYAKI BEEF. WAIT RIGHT HERE.
HE'S GETTING MORE AND MORE ANGRY
......
W-WHAT IS IT?

PUCKER
UH?!
GIVE ME A KISS. HOW ABOUT A KISS, PONTA-KUN?
BE A GOOD GIRL AND GIVE ME A KISSY. OKAY?
PET
PET
PET
WHAT IS HE DOING?
BEEP
BEEP
UH
GET OUT OF THE WAY! MOVE TO THE SIDE OF THE ROAD!
BEEP
BEEP
I CAN'T GET BY YOU
S-SORRY BUT MY ENGINE'S DIED.
JUST WAIT HERE A SECOND, OKAY?
POP-UP
I'LL PUSH.
I'LL HELP TOO.
ALL TOGETHER! PUSH!
PUSH!

AH.
ヴォォォッ
VROOM
ブォオォッ
ZOOM
ぐしゃっ
SMASH
HERE'S SOME MONEY FOR THE EGGS.
THAT'S OKAY. I'M FINE.
B-BUT...
1000
I'M SORRY, I'M SORRY.
I JUST STARTED DRIVING.
I WAS PLANNING ON MAKING DASHIMAKI EGGS ANYWAY.
BREAK THEM AND BEAT THEM. YOU SAVED ME A LOT OF WORK.
DASHIMAKI EGGS?
WHAT A STRANGE GUY.
HE DIDN'T LAUGH. HE DIDN'T WANT MONEY.

IT'S QUITE A COINCIDENCE THAT WE'RE BOTH GOING HOME THE SAME WAY, HUH?
HE'S A SURPRISINGLY GOOD GUY.
HAVE YOU EVER BEEN IN LOVE PONTA-KUN?
JUST LOITERING A LITTLE ALONG THE WAY.
SIGH
ハアー
FIRST LOVE...
WHY...
FIRST LOVE FOR ME, WHO DESPISES HUMANS...
SHE'S SO DIFFERENT FROM OTHER GIRLS. ANYWAY, I'M SURE IT'LL HAPPEN NATURALLY...
THAT'S RIGHT.
SHE'S GOT CRYSTAL CLEAR EYES LIKE YOU.
THOSE EYES...
PO...

SPRING
PONTA-SAN!!
I LOVE YOU!!
SORRY, SORRY.
NOBODY LIKES TO BE HUGGED ALL OF A SUDDEN.
HUFF HUFF
WATER UNDER THE BRIDGE.
SIGH
I'M SERIOUSLY ILL.
HE'S NOT A BAD GUY BUT,
HE IS WEIRD.
BUT IT DOES HAVE....
A GREAT SHAPE.
I MADE THESE IN HOME ECONOMICS.

SHE CERTAINLY...
GAVE IT HER ALL MAKING IT.
CHUCKLE...
IF SHE JUST DRESSED IT UP A LITTLE MORE...
RUSTLE
CLATTER
CLATTER
TROMP
TROMP
TROMP
...
TROMP
TROMP
SHUT UP! I CAN'T GET TO SLEEP!
IS THERE SOME MOUSE GOBLIN IN HERE?
TRAMP
TRAMP
TRAMP
TRAMP
SQUEAK SQUEAK

...1
2
3...
...
WHOA
THE CHOCOLATE HAD BABIES!
HOW CUTE
NO, NO! MITOSIS! ♡
THERE WAS ONLY ONE TO START WITH!
THAT MEANS ...
HA HA HA
HOW DID THEY MULTIPLY ?!
IT CAN'T BE!
TRAMP TRAMP
IS THERE SOME MOUSE GOBLIN IN HERE?
UH...
MOUSE POOP ...

GARBAGE COLLECTION SITE
STANDARD GARBAGE TUESDAY. THURSDAY. SATURDAY
SEPARATED GARBAGE FRIDAY
OVERSIZED GARBAGE
SNIFF SNIFF
SUSPECT
SUSPECT
SUSPECT
SORRY PONTA.
MIRAI-KUN ~~~~~~!
STUN
MORNING!
DID YOU TRY THE CHOCOLATE ~~~~~~?!
WELL THEN, LET'S GO!
SNIFF SNIFF
YE... YEAH.
WHISK
I SMELL CHOCOLATE !!!
PLOP

RUSTLE
RUSTLE
WHAT'S THIS ?!
SORRY !!
MOUSE POOP ?!
I COULD'VE TOLD RIGHT AWAY IF I SMELLED THEM.
SHHHHH SHHHHH
I CAN'T TELL THEM APART NO MATTER HOW MUCH I TRY.
I COULDN'T TELL.
MY NOSE ISN'T AS GOOD AS YOURS.
GLOOM

I'M REALLY SORRY.
I APOLOGIZE.
SO...
HUH?
......
DRAG
LOOK, DON'T BECOME A PIECE OF CHOCOLATE.
JUST CHANGING FROM DOG TO HUMAN IS CONFUSING ENOUGH.
MOPE MOPE
HEY, WHAT'S THAT?
IT'S JUST THAT I PUT A LOT...
A LOT OF MY FEELINGS OF LOVE INTO THAT CHOCOLATE.

THAT'S WHY
I WANTED TO EAT THEM SO BAD.
PAT PAT
ぽむぽむ
IT'S LIKE I'VE ALREADY EATEN T-THOSE FEELINGS!! SO DON'T FEEL DOWN.
REALLY? REALLY?
YEAH.
AND ANYWAY, THERE'S A LOT OF THINGS YOU LOVE RIGHT?
YEP.
JI-CHAN AND YUKA-CHAN
GRUB AND WALKS AND FRISBEE AND SUCH.
YEP, YEP.
BACK TO HER NORMAL SELF
SO YOU MEAN 'I LOVE MIRAI-KUN' IN THE SAME WAY, RIGHT?
THAT MAKES ME REALLY HAPPY.

FRISBEE...?
GRUB...?
WALKS...?
I ALSO...
LOVE YOU IN THE SAME SORT OF WAY.
THE SAME AS THOSE OTHER THINGS?
IT'S NOT LIKE THAT.
IT'S NOT LIKE THAT!
MY LOVE FOR YOU ISN'T THE SAME AS THOSE.
...PONTA?

MIRAI-KUN...
DO YOU KNOW...
WHEN I DECIDED I WANTED TO BECOME HUMAN?
WHEN I FIRST MET YOU.
HEY
SAY SOMETHING
A LOVE BETWEEN HUMANS AND DOGS CAN NEVER BE.
WELL THEN, I'M...
GONNA BECOME HUMAN!!!
IT'S AT THAT TIME,
I FELL IN LOVE WITH YOU!!

PAIN
ズキ…ン
PO...
FLING
DON'T TOUCH ME!

YOU'RE THROUGH MAKING THIS GIRL CRY.
THERE'S NO WAY I'LL LET THAT HAPPEN!!
THERE'S NO NEED TO STAND BY HIS SIDE ANYMORE.
LET'S GO.

WHEN I FIRST MET
YOU.
IT'S AT THAT TIME,
I FELL IN LOVE WITH YOU!!
WHAAAAAA!
SNIV...
SNIVEL.
......

DON'T ...
DON'T CRY ANYMORE.
START
NOT FOR THAT GUY.
THAT GUY...
WHAAAA!
OH, RATS! THAT HAD THE OPPOSITE EFFECT!
IF IT WAS ME...
ギュ
CLENCH
I WOULDN'T MAKE YOU CRY...
THERE'S NO WAY!
ドキン
THUMP
ドキン
THUMP
IT'S ONLY BEEN A FEW DAYS SINCE I'VE MET HER BUT...
I'VE HAD MY EYE ON HER THE WHOLE TIME...
DURING THAT TIME,

I'VE COME TO LIKE HER SO MUCH.
I WONDER IF SHE'LL GO OUT WITH ME?
I WONDER ...
IF SHE'LL LOVE ME...?
END OF CHAPTER 7

IDIOT
CHUCKLE

I DECIDED I WANTED TO BECOME HUMAN...
WHEN I FELL IN LOVE...
WITH YOU.

CHAPTER NUMBER 8

CHEEP CHEEP
チチチ…
BEEP BEEP
ピピ…
I…
LOVE YOU, MIRAI-KUN!
AH HA HA
YOU SAY IT SO INDIFFERENTLY, I DON'T BELIEVE YOU'RE SERIOUS.
DREAM
I AM SERIOUS.
YOU MIGHT BE SERIOUS BUT YOU'RE STILL A DOG!
WHAT A MESS I'VE MADE…
SINK

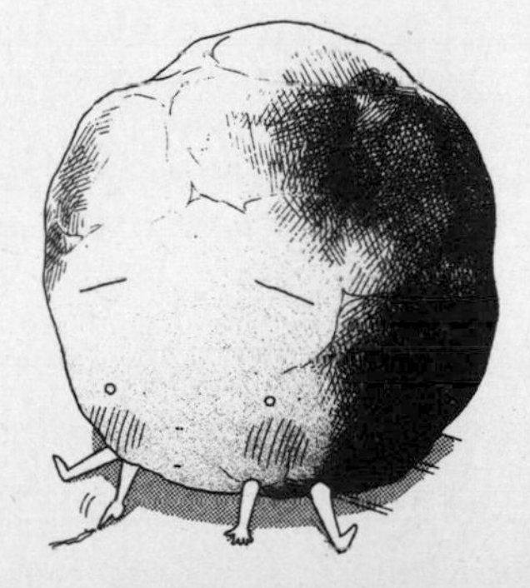

MOPE
MOPE

MOPE

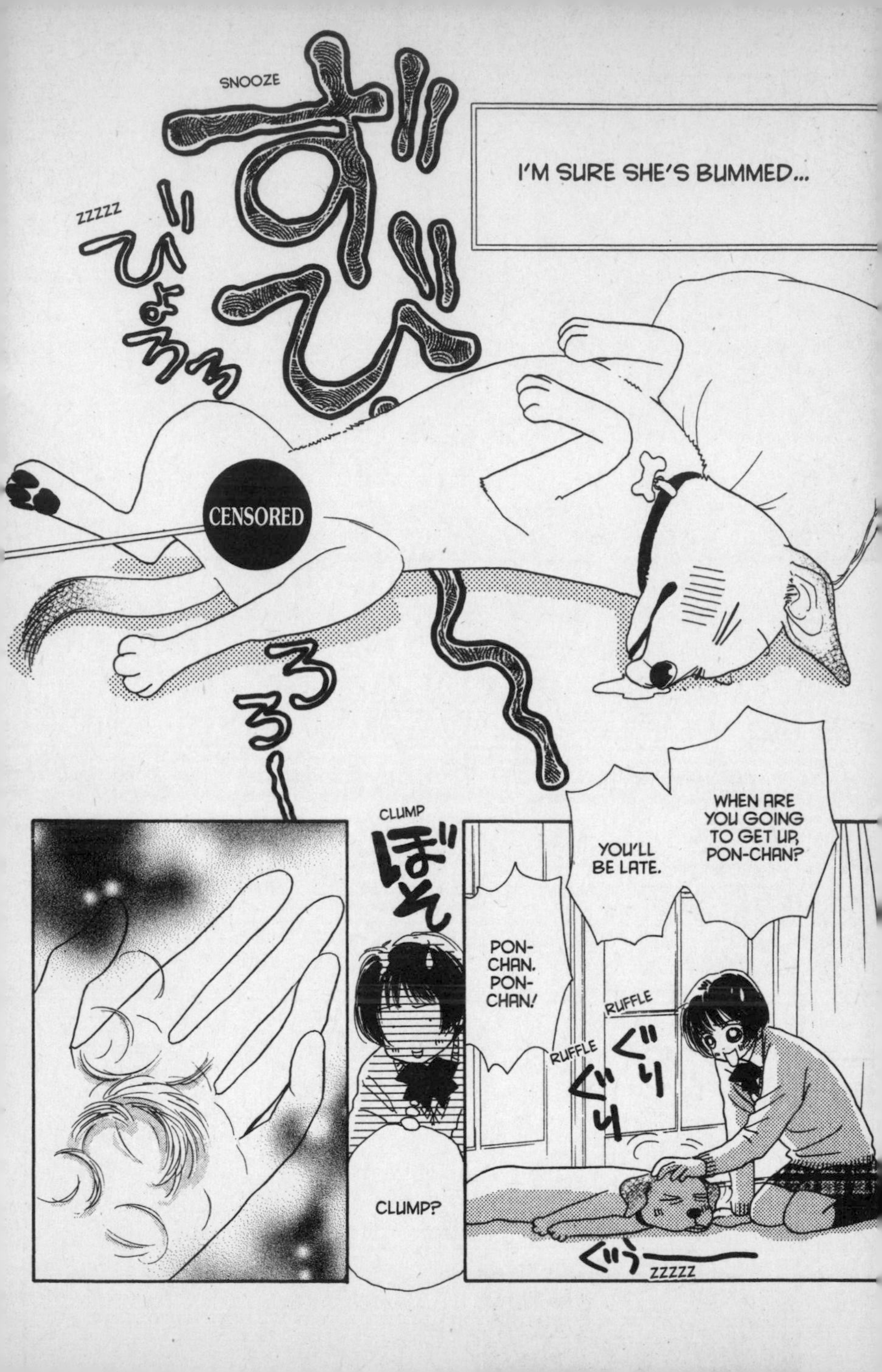
I'M SURE SHE'S BUMMED...
SNOOZE
ZZZZZ
CENSORED
WHEN ARE YOU GOING TO GET UP, PON-CHAN?
YOU'LL BE LATE.
PON-CHAN. PON-CHAN!
RUFFLE
RUFFLE
ZZZZZ
CLUMP
CLUMP?

PO...
PON-CHAN...
KOIZUMI.
LOOKS LIKE PONTA KOIZUMI'S ABSENT.
SHE'S SO BUMMED SHE'S NOT COMING TO SCHOOL?
BUT HER FACE DIDN'T SHOW THAT WHEN WE PARTED. THAT'S A LITTLE REASSURING...
RATTLE
FUJI-NAGA?!
I'M OUTTA HERE.
...

WHAT DO WE HAVE HERE?
IT'S ALOPECIA AREATA, CIRCULAR HAIR LOSS.
WHAT CAUSES IT?
DAZE ぽげ
LOOKING AT HER, I'D SAY STRESS.
VETERINARY
OSPITAL
I'LL GIVE YOU SOME OINTMENT BUT
THE BEST CURE IS TO GET RID OF THE SOURCE OF STRESS.
YOU'RE RIGHT!
IT'S TOTALLY SMOOTH HERE!
NATURALLY, SHE'S GOING BALD EVEN WHEN SHE'S HUMAN. →
AH HA HA
HOW INTERESTING!
IT DOESN'T LOOK INTERESTING
DAZE ぽげ
TELL ME, PON-CHAN!
DID SOMETHING TRAUMATIC HAPPEN?!
ぶんぶん WHZZZ
...
...じわ GUSH
PON-CHAN?
じょぼぼ WEEP WEEP

THAT'S RIGHT.
THERE WAS THAT THING ON VALENTINE'S DAY...
THE BEST CURE IS...
TO GET RID OF THE SOURCE OF STRESS.
CHEER UP, PON-CHAN.
IT CAN'T BE THAT TRAUMATIC.
AFTER ALL, MIRAI-KUN SAID HE LIKED YOU, RIGHT?!
MAYBE THAT DOESN'T MEAN LOVE BUT
HE DOESN'T HATE YOU!
PLOOP
POP
...
MIRAI-KUN REALLY LIKES YOU SO THERE'S NO REASON TO CRY!!
PLOOP
POP
YOU...
PLOOP
YOU THINK SO?
SHE'S ALMOST BACK TO HER OLD SELF!
I DO!
PLOP
POP
UH, WHAT ABOUT YOU, YUKA-CHAN?
HUH
DID YOU GIVE SOMETHING TO MIRAI-KUN?

YOU DIDN'T ?!
I GAVE SOMETHING... BUT NOT TO MIRAI-KUN...
UH... A GUY IN MY CLASS.
MUTTER
MUTTER
DO YOU HATE MIRAI-KUN?!
IT'S NOT THAT...
I UNDERSTOOD CLEARLY AT THE HATSU-MODE...
THAT I ADORE MIRAI-KUN.
ADORE?
NOT LOVE.
OHH.
SO, DO YOU LOVE THE GUY YOU GAVE A VALENTINE TO?
BLUSH
WE'RE TALKING ABOUT YOU NOW, PON-CHAN!
HEY, CHEER UP, PON-CHAN!
WHAT MAKES YOU SO CHARMING, PON-CHAN, IS YOUR CHEERFULNESS.
CHEERFULNESS. ...?
YEAH!
IF I'M CHEERFUL, MAYBE MIRAI-KUN WILL COME AROUND.
THAT'S IT!!
FULL-BLOOM

IF I'M CHEERFUL !!
AH!
DING DONG
COULD THAT BE MIRAI-KUN?!
COMING !
WHAT IF MIRAI-SAN'S ACTUALLY HAVING SECOND THOUGHTS ABOUT PON-CHAN?
MAYBE I ENCOURAGED HER TOO MUCH? BUT I DID WANT HER TO CHEER UP.
...
GO-KUN?!
WOW
FLOWERS FOR ME?!
OH, WELL I THOUGHT YOU WERE SICK AND...
THE GUY WHO KNOCKED MIRAI-SAN DOWN.
THAT GUY FROM THE HATSUMODE.
AREN'T YOU GOING TO SCHOOL, YUKA-CHAN?
I'M STILL NOT READY.
DOESN'T WANT TO SHOW HER FACE TO GO-KUN.
G-GO AHEAD.
AH, PON-CHAN!

A HAT? BUT WHY?
WHY, YOU ASK? UM...
TO HIDE YOUR BALD SPOT.
...
WELL... UH...
IT'S A CHARM TO HELP THINGS GO WELL WITH MIRAI-KUN.
WHOA!
SO DON'T TAKE IT OFF, NO MATTER WHAT.
GOT IT! SEE YOU LATER!
I WONDER IF THAT GUY...
LIKES PONTA...?
I DON'T EXPECT HE KNOWS...
SHE'S A DOG.
SCARY
HOW...
HE'S GOT IT BAD
SKI-IP
すきーっぷ
CHEERFULLY, CHEERFULLY.
HOW CAN SHE BE SO CUTE!
SKI-IP
すきーっぷ
SOME-HOW...
I'VE...
GOT THE URGE TO SKIP TOO.

SLAM
SKIP TO MY LOO, MY DAR-LING ~ !!
UH?
SKIP TO MY LOO...
LOO LOO, SKIP TO MY LOO. LOO LOO,
......
GOOD MORNING, MIRAI-KUN !!!
CHEER-FULLY !!!
!!

SHE'S FEELING BETTER.
WHAT A RELIEF.
THAT WAS A LITTLE SCARY BUT...
SNICKER.
AND I'M THE ONE WHO HELPED HER BOUNCE BACK
I BROUGHT HER HERE TO BOOT!
HMPH.
NAUSEOUS
OH YEAH!
ぐるぐる
TWIRL
TWIRL
LOOK! LOOK ~~~ !!
HUH ?!
ぐるぐる
TWIRL
LOOK, I'M CHEERFUL !!
PO-PO-PONTA-SAN !!
DON'T USE THE PANEL BORDER AS A GIANT SWING!
NO, I MEAN ...!
DON'T CAUSE A RUCKUS DURING CLASS!!!
IT'S MOST ABSURD TO WEAR A HAT INDOORS!!
WHISK
ぱっ
AH!

DON'T!
GIVE IT BACK!
WHAT...?
IF IT'S OKAY WITH YOU...
I MADE A PROMISE TO YUKA-CHAN.
HMPH!
WHO'S YUKA-CHAN ?!
IT'S AGAINST THE RULES !!

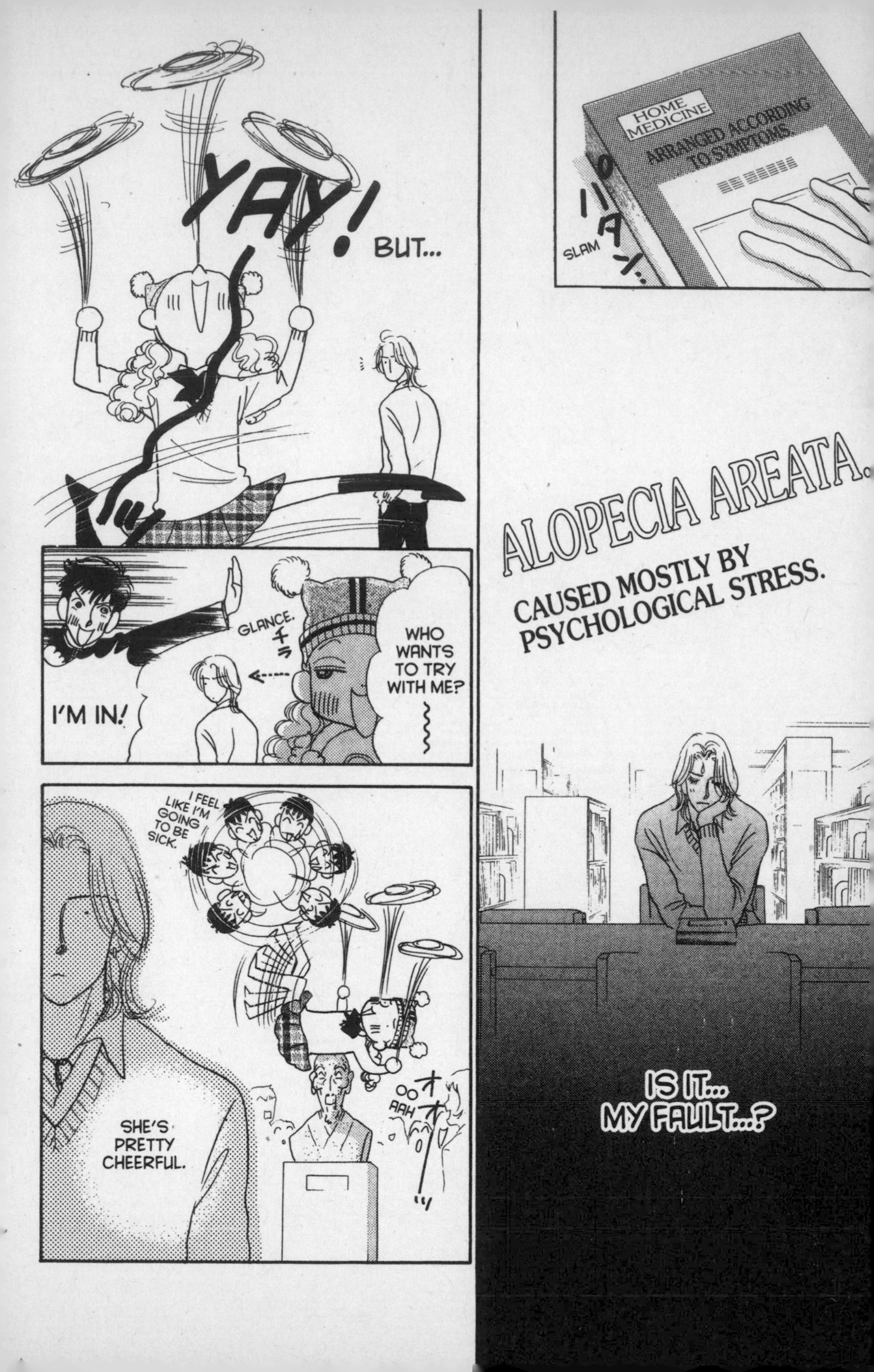
HOME MEDICINE
ARRANGED ACCORDING TO SYMPTOMS.
SLAM
ALOPECIA AREATA.
CAUSED MOSTLY BY PSYCHOLOGICAL STRESS.
IS IT... MY FAULT...?
YAY!
BUT...
GLANCE.
WHO WANTS TO TRY WITH ME?
I'M IN!
I FEEL LIKE I'M GOING TO BE SICK.
AAH
SHE'S PRETTY CHEERFUL.

TRAMP
TRAMP
TRAMP
KYA! KYA!
LOOK, SHE SEEMS SO CHEERFUL.
WAIT FOR ME!
DASH
...
I'VE GOT YOU!
BLISSFUL.
KYA! KYA!
PONTA-SAN, YOU'RE ALMOST A LITTLE TOO CHEERFUL.
WELL, THAT'S JUST...
KYA HA HA HA
HOW I AM!
AH HA HA HA

I'M JUST TOO CHEERFUL.
チラ
GLANCE
SHE'S CHEERFUL AS ALL GET OUT BUT...
AM I A FOOL...
FOR WORRYING ...?
...
PONTA-SAN.
SOMEHOW...
SOMEHOW IT SEEMS LIKE I'M
MORE DISTANT FROM MIRAI-KUN THAN BEFORE.

FLUTTER
…ぽそっ
AH!
IT'S GOTTEN HUGE...
...
OH NO! MY HAT!

FROM SOMEONE WHO KNOWS NOTHING!

IKEZAWA
MC
THANK YOU FOR READING VOLUME 2!
WELL THEN, HOW ARE EVERYBODY'S DOGS? BOTH OF MINE ARE WELL. THE OTHER DAY, SOMEONE SAID ONE WAS TOO FAT (40 KG) SO I PUT HIM ON A DIET. HE'S DOWN TO 37 KG NOW BUT THAT'S STILL HUGE (HA HA).
RAISING THE TWO OF THEM AT THE SAME TIME HAS MADE ME REALIZE MORE AND MORE THAT DOGS HAVE THEIR OWN PERSONALITY AND CHARACTER. PONTA HAS A "FIRST SON" PERSONALITY AND HE HAS STRONG SELF-CONTROL AND A PRIZE TEMPERAMENT. HE LIKES TO PLAY WITH OTHER DOGS. HE GETS EXCITED WHEN HE SEES A CAT AND DASHES OFF. HE LOOKS LIKE A BIG IDIOT WHEN HE SLEEPS AND WHEN I ENTER THE ROOM, HE BARKS AS IF TO SAY, 'WHO GOES THERE?' IT'S A LITTLE AGGRAVATING.
SCAREDY CAT.
I ALMOST FORGOT, BUT HIS SNORING IS SOMETHING TO BEHOLD!
ON THE OTHER HAND, GUTS IS LIKE THE SECOND SON AND HAS THE TEMPERAMENT OF THE BABY OF THE FAMILY. LIKE A SPOILED CHILD HE'LL IMMEDIATELY WHINE LIKE, 'LET ME OUT!' OR 'FEED ME!'. HIS 'PET ME!' ATTACK IS ALSO FIERCE. HE LIKES PLAYING WITH OTHER OWNERS MORE THAN OTHER DOGS. HE'S GOT A LOT OF MOXY SO HE DOESN'T GET PARTICULARLY WORKED UP WHEN HE COMES ACROSS OTHER DOGS OR CATS. HE DOESN'T SNORE BUT, ON TOP OF MAKING LOUD NOISES WHEN HE BREATHES, THAT BREATH STINKS (PEE YOO!)

LET ME KNOW WHAT YOUR DOG'S PERSONALITY IS LIKE, EVERYONE! SEE YOU!!

SORRY! SORRY!
I'VE DONE IT AGAIN.
IT'S JUST THAT YOU'RE WEARING THE SAME HAT AS HER.
HMPH!
PONTA-KUN, DO YOU LIVE LIFE TO THE FULLEST EVERY DAY?
RIGHT NOW, I'M LIVING LIFE TO THE FULLEST LIKE THERE'S NO TOMORROW.
HUH?! WHY'S THAT?!
IT'S NO SECRET! IT'S BECAUSE I'M BY PONTA-SAN'S SIDE!!
AH, NOT YOU, THE HUMAN PONTA. OF COURSE, I LIKE YOU TOO BUT...
AAH, IT'S GREAT TO BE ALIVE!
LOVE IS THE GREATEST!
I LOVE...
PONTA-SAAAN!
YOOOOOOUUUU!!

I LOVE YOU SOOOO MUCH!!!
I'M A HAPPY GUY!
GO EXEMPLIFIES THE PHRASE, 'IGNORANCE IS BLISS'.
PANT PANT PANT
ME?
IF I MET PONTA WITHOUT KNOWING SHE'S A DOG...
HA HA HA, YOU'RE A FRIENDLY ONE.
...

WHAT AM I SAYING...

PAIN

OUCH.
SHEESH
WHY IS MY STOMACH HURTING ALL OF A SUDDEN?
WOOF
WOOF
WOOF
HEY! THERE'S A LABRADOR OVER THERE.
LAB?
OU...
OUCH, OUCH ...
I NEED SOME GASTER-10.
WOBBLE

DATE?
UH, NO, THAT WOULD BE BLOWING IT OUT OF PROPORTION.
I THOUGHT IT'D BE NICE TO TAKE A SIDE TRIP ON THE WAY HOME OCCASIONALLY.
IF YOU DIDN'T HAVE OTHER PLANS...
GLANCE
NOTHING IN PARTI-CULAR.
OKAY, THEN IT'S DECIDED!
...
...MIRAI-KUN...
HEY! THERE'S A SWEET SMELL IN THE AIR!!
TWITCH TWITCH
PONTA-SAN, LET'S GET ONE!
THAT'S MIRAI-KUN'S SCENT!!
SNIFF SNIFF
AND THERE IT IS, A CREPE STAND!!
CREPES
CREPES
109
PIA
WHIRL

THERE'S NO REASON TO BELIEVE HE'S HERE.
I ONLY SMELL CREPES.
SCENT?
......
WHAT AM I DOING...?
ANYWAY, LETS GO.
I'M NOT A STALKER !!
OH NO, WHERE ARE THEY?
OUCH.
NOT AGAIN.
NOT HERE.
NOT HERE.

シネフレ
落雷と共にそれは蘇った
WHEN LIGHTNING STRIKES, IT COMES BACK FROM THE DEAD.
ザ・ゾンビ
THE ZOMBIE
RAKUSHO BROTHERS FILM
上映中
......
WHEN LIGHTNING STRIKES
MUNCH
MUNCH
MUNCH
I GOT US SOME COLA TOO.
THIS IS DELICIOUS, HUH?
IT'S NO BIG DEAL FOR HIM TO WATCH THAT.
CAN I HELP YOU?
THIS IS BAD.
UUGH.
THIS HAD TO HAPPEN NOW.
ONE...
ONE STUDENT TICKET, PLEASE.

WHIMPER
CUTE DOG, HUH PONTA-SAN?
WHIMPER
WHIMPER
SNIFF SNIFF
!!
IF YOU DON'T WATCH, YOU WON'T UNDERSTAND WHAT'S GOING ON.
I'm going to wake up Papa,
who's sleeping in his grave.
ぼく、お墓に眠ってる
パパを起こしに行くよ
Michael! Papa is dead!
マイケル！
パパは死んだのよ!!
MUNCH MUNCH
MUNCH
PONTA-SAN'S TOUGH.
I'M HERE CRYING AND SHE'S...
I HAVE NO IDEA WHAT'S GOING ON.
DARN, I CAN'T SEE.
You'll never see him again.

RUMBLE
FLASH
RUMBLE
PONTA-SAN?
OH NO!
WHERE'S PONTA?
WHERE IS SHE ?!
CRASH

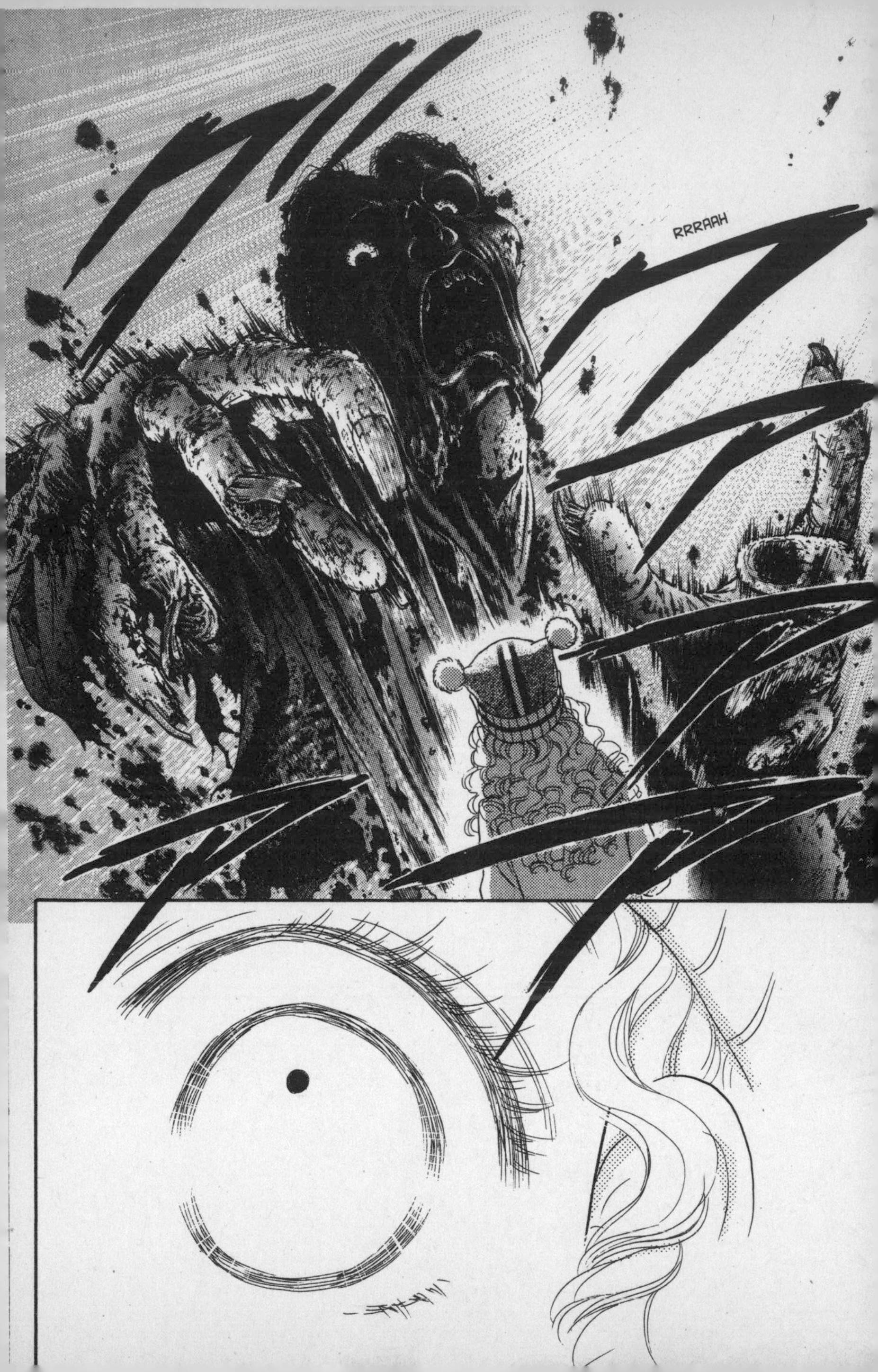
RRRAAH

KYAAAAAA~!

PO-
PONTA-SAN?!
WHAT WAS THAT?
KYA
OUCH! SOME-ONE STEPPED ON MY FOOT.
WHAH
WHSSSH
KYAA!
A D...
DOG...
A DOG! THERE'S A DOG IN HERE!
WHAAH
HELP!
RUN!
KYA
ZOMBIES ARE FINE BUT NOT DOGS!

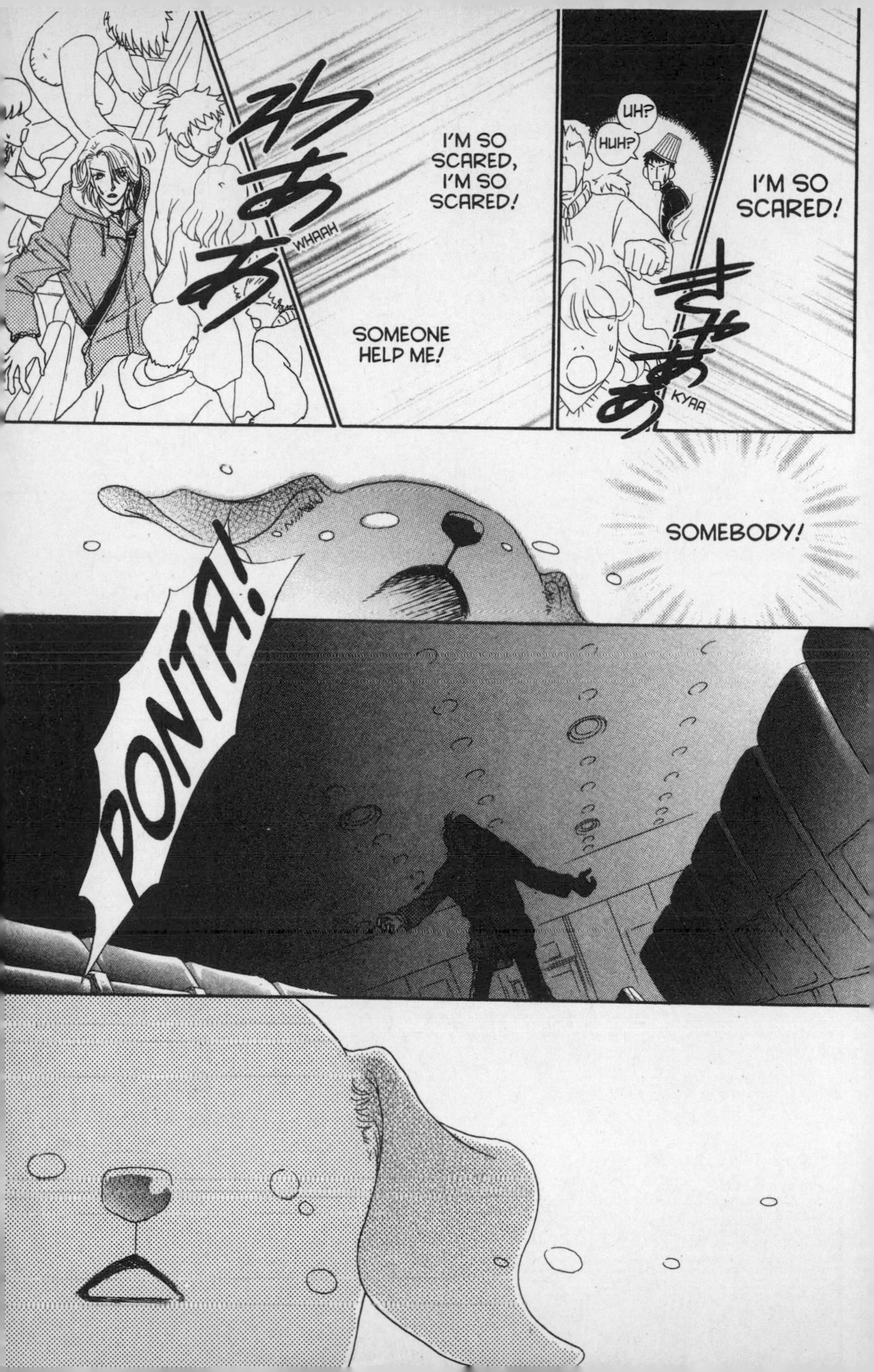
UH?
HUH?
I'M SO SCARED!
きゃああ
KYAA
わああ
WHAAH
I'M SO SCARED, I'M SO SCARED!
SOMEONE HELP ME!
SOMEBODY!
PONTA!

MIRAI-
KUN.

...
ピカッ
FLASH

YOU'RE ALL RIGHT NOW.
DON'T BE SCARED.
NOW I UNDER-STAND...
WHAT WAS GOING ON.
SHALL I GET YOUR HAT BACK?
WE'VE GOT TO HIDE YOUR HEAD.

OHH...
MIRAI-KUN!
WHAT'S WRONG ?!
HEY!

MIRAI-
KUN!

THIS TIME, I'LL HELP YOU.
HOLD ON TO ME, MIRAI-KUN.
I'M SORRY.
I CAN'T LOVE YOU, GO-KUN.
IT'S JUST THAT,
MY REASON FOR BEING HUMAN...
IS MY LOVE FOR MIRAI-KUN.
SO...
I'M SORRY.
CRUMPLE
へにゃ…
I CAN'T BELIEVE IT...
I HATE HUMANS, AND THE FIRST PERSON I FALL IN LOVE WITH TURNS OUT TO BE A DOG!

うおあぁっあっおっ
WHAAAH
THUD
ゴン
THUD
ゴン
THUD
ゴンッ
GET A HOLD OF YOURSELF, GO!
THIS CAN'T BE HAPPENING!
HAVE YOU FORGOT HOW YOU'RE ALWAYS BEING TRICKED AND LAUGHED AT?!
THAT'S IT! I'M EASILY TRICKED!
THAT WAS ALL A TRICK! YEAH! A TRICK!
NOTHING BUT A TRICK!
NEUROTIC GASTRITIS?
WHAT'S THAT?
IT'S THE SAME THING THAT CAUSED YOUR BALDNESS.
HOW PITIFUL...
OUCH. IT STILL HURTS.
HMM...
WHAT A PITY...
AT LEAST MY BALDNESS DOESN'T HURT.
しょぼん…
BUMMED
POOR MIRAI-KUN.
BUT YOU CRIED.

AND IT WAS PAINFUL.
I'M SORRY...
WHETHER DOG OR HUMAN...
PONTA IS PONTA.
I DIDN'T HAVE THE COURAGE TO RESPOND TO YOUR 'I LOVE YOU'.
COURAGE?
YEAH.
NORMALLY, THAT KIND OF COURAGE DOESN'T COME OUT.
BUT IT'S SO GREAT THAT IF IT DOESN'T COME OUT, IT BECOMES 'NEUROTIC GASTRITIS'.

I SEE.
IT WAS THAT GREAT, HUH...?
THAT'S RIGHT.
HMMM
WHY?!
COLLAPSE
I THINK I'M GONNA DIE
MIRAI IWAKI, AGE 17.
THE ROAD TO PERVERSION HAS NOW ONLY JUST BEGUN.
IT'S ALL A TRICK!
I KNOW IT IS
END OF CHAPTER 8

CHAPTER
NUMBER
9
I'LL HELP YOU OUT!

SNOOZE
ZZZZZ
CENSORED

WHOOSH

THAT WAS GREAT ~~~ !!
GREAT, GREAT, GREAT !!
CLAP
パチ
CLAP
パチ
CLAP
パチ
IT'S BEEN A WHILE, BUT SURPRIS-INGLY I HAVEN'T LOST MY TOUCH.
HEH HEH
WANT TO TRY?
YEAH !!
OKAY, WATCH ME AND I'LL SHOW YOU HOW IT'S DONE.

SQUAT DOWN AND LOWER YOUR CENTER OF GRAVITY.
AND TO TURN...
PANT
PANT
PANT
WHAT'S WITH THE 'PANT PANT'?
I HAVE NO IDEA HOW WE'RE SUPPOSED TO SKATE TOGETHER!
←BAILED.
KYA!
KYA!
IT'S JUST THAT—
IT'S JUST THAT WHAT?!
ぴと
SNUGGLE
I WANTED TO CUDDLE WITH YOU, MIRAI-KUN.
I GUESS ...

I GUESS IT CAN'T BE HELPED.
I CAN'T BELIEVE THIS...
SPRING'S IN FULL BLOOM.
AND THE LOVE BETWEEN THE TWO OF THEM IS ALSO IN FULL BLOOM. ...♡
OOWHOA! ~
SHE SAYS THIS BUT IT'S NO SURPRISE SHE'S WANTED TO TRY THIS.
HEY, WE'RE HERE.
RATTLE
I'M GOING IN, PONTA.
MIRAI-KUUN! ~
I CAN'T STOP ~!
SSSSHHHH
KYA HA HA HA
WHAT ?!

WHOOSH
OH NO.
CRASH
YOU...
I CAN'T BELIEVE YOU...
AH
THE V... VASE...

RATTLE
I HOPE NOTHING HAPPENED TO THE VASE ~~~~~~!
SCAMPER
VASE...?
VASE...?
YEAH.
I'M LOOKING AFTER IT FOR SOME RELATIVES.
THEY ASKED ME TO KEEP IT HERE BECAUSE THEIR BABY STARTED WALKING AND THEY DON'T WANT IT BROKEN.
WHEW
W-WHAT A RELIEF...

WHY DON'T THEY WANT IT BROKEN?
MAYBE, BECAUSE IT'S SUPER EXPEN-SIVE.
EXPEN-SIVE...?
チッ チッ
IT COSTS A LOT OF MONEY, OKAY?
IF IT WAS BROKEN AT MY HOUSE, I'D BE...
!!
WHAHOO.
LOOKS LIKE A CIRCUS PERFORMER.
THIS IS A VASE! NOT A SKATEBOARD!!
IT'S NOT A TOY!
IT'S A DECORATION TO LOOK AT!
YOU'RE PROBABLY HUNGRY. I'LL BRING BACK SOMETHING TO EAT SO JUST BEHAVE YOURSELF AND WAIT.
ALL RIGHT?!
......
LOOKING.
FOCUS じ
LOOKING.
FOCUS じ
SPIDER
!!
SPIDER

A S-SPIDER!
NOOO!
AND IT'S MOVING!
WHISK WHISK
かしかしかしっ
...
PLUNG
がばっ
BANG
ゴキ
I CAN'T GET IN THERE.
OUCH
!!!
PERHAPS
SMOOCH
ちゅううう
POO-WOOF
ぼわわわ〜ん

PLUNG
GIGGLE
SCAMPER
SCAMPER
HELP ME
UGH.
YIKES!
THAT TICKLES!
STRUGGLE
STRUGGLE
......
UH?
......
U...
WHISK
WHISK
......

PONTA, HERE'S SOME POTATO...
POTETO
WHAT ARE YOU DOING ?!
I CAN'T BELIEVE YOU WENT SO FAR AS TO TRANSFORM !
COME ON! GIVE ME THAT VASE!
OUCH, OUCH.
I THOUGHT I TOLD YOU THIS WASN'T A TOY!
WHIZZZ
WHAT THE ?!

THUMP
どでん
YOU CAN'T...
...GET THE VASE OFF?
...
コク
NOD
YOUR HEAD GOT STUCK RIGHT?
NOD NOD
コクコク
H-HELP ME, MIRAI-KUN.
NOD NOD
フラフラ
OH, NOT THAT WAY...
SLIP

IKEBANA
↓
IKE-PONTA
STRUGGLE
じたばた
STRUGGLE
じたばた
PUH HA HA.
AH
HEY...
THIS ISN'T SOMETHING
TO LAUGH ABOUT.
UGH.
QUIVER
ブルルッ
I'VE GOTTA GO...
SCRAMBLE
AAH, PONTA!
SHATTER
ガシャーンッ

AAH
WHIZ
ショワワ～
AH-HEM
DON'T LOOK, OKAY?
IF YOU HAVE TO GO, JUST SAY SO.
...OH YEAH, SHE'S A DOG, SHE CAN'T.
IT'S TIMES LIKE THESE...
SCRUNCH
ず～ん
THAT THE REALITY OF PONTA BEING A DOG WEIGHS MOST HEAVILY ON ME.
CAN'T BLAME HIM.
YOU DONE?
ポカポカ
WARM SUNNY
PONTA?
WHY ARE YOU SO CALM?
HEY, WHY...?

SHE'S STARTING TO SUFFOCATE
!!
ARE YOU IN PAIN?
NO MATTER HOW EXPENSIVE THIS VASE IS...
HANG IN THERE!
ALL RIGHT, THIS'LL HURT A LITTLE SO JUST BITE THE BULLET.
IT CAN'T TAKE THE PLACE OF PONTA'S LIFE!
SMASH
CRACK

SPLIT
WHEW
YOU'RE A LIFE-SAVER!
YOU'RE A LIFE-SAVER!
ESCAPING SPIDER.
YOUR... FACE...
WHAT ?
PU HA HA HA
IT'S VASE SHAPED ~ !

OO HA HA HA HA HA HA HA
うははははは
ANYWAY, EVERY-THING'S ALL RIGHT. EVERY-THING'S ALL RIGHT.
EVERY-THING'S ALL RIGHT.
BUT...
THAT CAN'T BE SAID FOR EVERYTHING.
FOCUS
じ
WE CAN'T HAVE FUN FOR A WHILE SO YOU'LL HAVE TO BEAR WITH ME, PONTA,
RATS! IT HAD TO BE DURING SPRING BREAK...
EVEN WHEN TRANS-FORMED, HER HEAD'S SHAPED LIKE A VASE.
WHY?!
BEFORE YOU ASK WHY, FIRST, FIX YOUR FACE.

WHY CAN'T WE HAVE FUN?
PART TIME JOB.
I HAVE TO PAY FOR THE VASE.
PART TIME JOB?
OHH, YOU HAVE NO IDEA WHAT I MEAN.
HELP WANTED
INQUIRE INSIDE.
HEY! IT SAYS, 'HELP WANTED. INQUIRE INSIDE.'
YOU WORK AT THIS SORT OF PLACE AND YOU GET MONEY.
AND WITH THAT MONEY...
I WANT TO DO IT TOO! I WANT A PART TIME JOB!
WHA HA HA HA HA
THAT'S FUNNY! THAT'S NOT FOR YOU!
WHAT ?!
? ??
WHY ?
OH!
HERE'S AN-OTHER ONE.
HELP WANTED
11-7P.M.
850 YEN*/HOUR.
AND HERE TOO.
AND OVER THERE TOO!
アルバイト
パート募集
SWIVEL
キョロ
SWIVEL
キョロ
SHE'S HAPPY TO READ HER FIRST WORDS.
THERE'S QUITE A FEW PART TIME JOBS.
MIRAI-KUN?
ANTIQUE SHOP

*ABOUT $8.30

¥250,000-
I GOT IT!
WE'LL WORK AND GET MONEY...
YOU DON'T GET IT...
AND THEN, WE CAN BUY THIS ONE!
MIRAI-KUN?
AH! THE SAME ONE!
YOU DON'T HOW HARD IT IS TO EARN 250,000 YEN* WITH A JOB LIKE THIS!
THAT'S NOT THE SORT OF THING TO LAUGH ABOUT AND SAY LIKE IT'S FUN!!
*ABOUT $2,430.
UHHH, A GOOD PAYING JOB...
GOOD PAYING JOB...
FLIP
FLIP
OH, YOU GOTTA BE KIDDING ME!

I'M SORRY.
RUSTLE
ぽふ
IT'S ONLY NATURAL THAT YOU DON'T UNDERSTAND ABOUT JOBS AND MONEY.
SORRY I GOT ANGRY.
HEY,
I CAN MANAGE, SO...
DON'T WORRY.
BUT...
MIRAI-KUN'S FACE SAYS HE'S IN TROUBLE...

I WANT TO HELP MIRAI-KUN!
J
PART-TIME JOB
O
B
にかっ GRIN
PLEASE GIVE ME A JOB!!
COMMOTION
ざわ ざわ
KYA
キャ
WHA HA HA
わはは
UH... UM...
SWIVEL
キョロ
SWIVEL
キョロ
I WANT A 'GOOD PAYING JOB'.
WHAT DO WE HAVE HERE? YOU'RE A CUTE GIRL
BUT DO YOU KNOW WHAT KIND OF PLACE THIS IS?
A PLACE TO EAT DELICIOUS FOOD...I THINK?
GO HOME KID!
HULLABALOO
HEART THROB LOUNGE. LOVE LOVE JEWELRY.
YEOUCH

HOW CRUEL!
OUCH
SO, YOU'RE LOOKING FOR SOMETHING TO DO?
HUH?
DOO-DOO?
AH HA HA, THAT'S FUNNY. NO, AS AN ESCORT.
AN ESCORT.
ESCORT...?
ANOTHER JOKE BUT YOU KNOW WHAT I'M TALKING ABOUT.
AN ESCORT.
SOMEONE THAT HELPS SOMEONE IN NEED.
SOMEONE IN NEED...
SOMEONE IN NEED EQUALS MIRAI-KUN.
YOU'LL HELP ME?!

AAH, ALL YOU HAVE TO DO IS HAVE DINNER WITH ME AND I'LL GIVE YOU MONEY.
REALLY ?!
SAFETY FIRST
SAFETY FIRST
NEW GUY!
OVER HERE WHEN YOU'RE DONE.
HURRY UP
YEAH, YEAH.
UGH...

PONTA
?
HEY!
ガッ
CLASP
WHAT'RE YOU DOING STANDING AROUND SPACING OUT?!
HAH?!
KNEAD
もみ
KNEAD
もみ
KNEAD
もみ
HE'S HUGE.
CLANK
CLANK
THAT CREEP!
GET THE LEAD OUT!
I'M HERE SWALLOWING MY TEARS, WORKING AND SHE'S OUT HAVING A NIGHT OUT ON THE TOWN.
CRAP!
WHEEZE
ハァ
WHEEZE
ハァ
WHEEZE
IT'S HARD TO IMAGINE A DOG HAVING A NIGHT ON THE TOWN.

YOU'RE GIVING ME THIS MUCH?!
THIS IS GREAT FOR JUST EATING TOGETHER.
THIS ESCORT STUFF IS A GOOD JOB!
AH HA HA. YOU'RE JUST EXAGGER-ATING.
SHE SAYS THIS WITHOUT CONSIDERING THE AMOUNT, JUST THE NUMBER OF BILLS (HA HA)
BUT DEPENDING ON WHAT YOU WANT TO DO...
YOU CAN GET MORE MONEY...?
OKAY THEN, SEE YOU LATER OJI-SAN!
BYE BYE
I DON'T KNOW... BUT SHE'S A REMARKABLY CHEERFUL GIRL.
WELL, THAT'S FINE.
SHE SEEMS GAME...
HEH HEH
LA DEE DAH.
PONTA, YOU GOT A JOB?!
YOU HELPED ME SO MUCH, THANK YOU.

I'LL DO A LOT MORE OF THIS PAID ESCORT THING
AND GET A LOT MORE MONEY...
AND I'LL HELP OUT MIRAI-KUN A LOT! ...♡
GRRR
THAT CREEP'S STILL AT IT.
ARE YOU STILL...
SLACKING OFF?
YOU WANNA GO A FEW ROUNDS WITH ME? AH?

CLANK
CLANK
CLANK
CLANK
CLANK
CLANK
CLANK
I UNDERSTAND THAT I'M BORED AND CAN'T HAVE FUN BUT...
CLANK
SHE DOESN'T HAVE TO GO ON SOME KIND OF DATE WITH THAT MIDDLE AGE MAN.
HOW 'BOUT IT?
BURP

IT CAN'T BE.
I WANT A JOB TOO!!
LBEST
HOTEL エンペラー2
ムール
HOTEL M
HOTEL ア♥ムール
HOTEL α
HOTEL
NEWマーキュリー
THAT FOOL.
GRAB

HEY! I'M TIRED OF YOU SCREWING AROUND ON THE JOB!
ARE YOU REALLY GOING TO GIVE A LOT MORE MONEY THAN YESTERDAY FOR JUST HAVING A REST WITH YOU?!
INFORMATION
REST 4500 YEN*
LODGING 6800 YEN**
HOTEL
*ABOUT $44. **ABOUT $66.
I'M NOT SCREWING AROUND
BUT...
MY GIRLFRIEND'S CHASTITY CAN'T BE RECOVERED !!
BOSS !
THUD

OH, HIS GIRL-FRIEND? MUST'VE MADE HER CRY.
YOU'VE GOT A BUMP ON YOUR HEAD, BOSS.
PLUNK
ぼふ
A REST ~~~~~!
IT'S SO FLUFFY! ~
KYA HA HA HA
ぼいん
BOING
ぼいん
BOING
HOTEL
エンペラー2
PONTA ─!!
HOTEL
HOTEL
61 HOTEL
NEW マーキュリー

SWIVEL
くるッ
AH!
LET'S TAKE A LITTLE REST, OKAY?
YEAH!
A REST!
......
......
?
....
SWIVEL
くるッ
PLUNK
HUH ?!

WHAT ARE YOU DOING, OJI-SAN!?
YOU KNOW EXACTLY WHAT I'M DOING.
WE'RE HAVING A REST,♡ RIGHT?
なでなで GROPE GROPE
T-THIS ISN'T HAVING A REST!
OOH
I LIKE A LITTLE FIGHT.
GRIP
グイ
IT GETS ME IN THE MOOD.
NO...
NO.

うちゅるぅ～!!
SMOOCH
STOP IT!!!!
HUH?
WHAT'S THIS?!

WHAT DO WE HAVE HERE?!
......
HUH...
I-I'M...
GRIN
GRASP
OH, COSTUME PLAY
I WOULD'VE PREFERRED A BUNNY BUT...
I LIKE A CUTE DOG COSTUME AS WELL.
NOOOO—!

BANG
THWACK
YOU PERVERTED CREEP !!

WHEEZE ハア
WHEEZE ハア
WHEEZE ハア
ハア
PONTA...
DO YOU KNOW WHAT YOU WERE DOING?
...ESCORT...
YOU...
KNEW ABOUT THAT?!
HE SAID AN ESCORT HELPS PEOPLE...
I...
WANTED TO HELP YOU, MIRAI-KUN.

IF I GOT A LOT OF MONEY...
I THOUGHT I WOULD BE ABLE TO HELP YOU.

I CAN'T BELIEVE YOU...
YOU'RE SOME PIECE OF WORK
PINCH
むにっ
YOU'RE REALLY SOME PIECE OF WORK!
むに
PINCH
PINCH
むにむに
PINCH

CONTINUED IN GURU GURU PON-CHAN 3

DELICIOUS!
ウマイ〜ッ

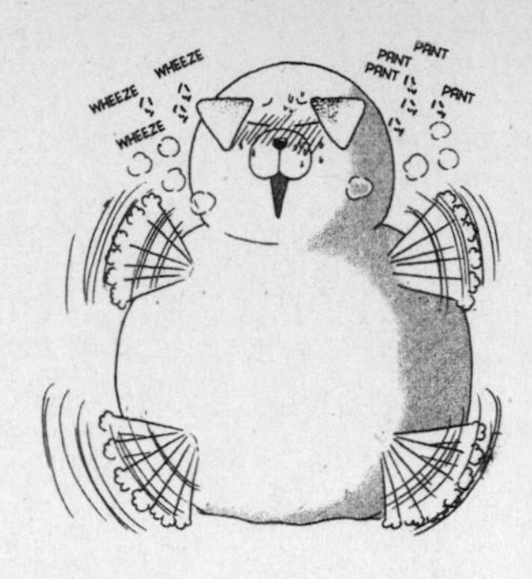
WHEEZE WHEEZE WHEEZE
PANT PANT PANT PANT

LICK
ペろ…

WOBBLE
フラ
WOBBLE
フラ

WHEEZE WHEEZE WHEEZE
PANT PANT PANT PANT

About the Creator

Satomi Ikezawa, a prolific manga-ka, finished *Guru Guru Pon-chan* in 2000. She is currently working on *Othello,* which is being serialized in the Kodansha weekly manga magazine, *Bessatsu Friend.*

Ikezawa won the 24th Kodansha Manga Prize in 2000 for *Guru Guru Pon-chan.*

She has two Labradors, named Guts and Ponta. Both are male, despite the Ponta of *Guru Guru Pon-Chan* being a girl.

Translation Notes

Japanese is a tricky language for most Westerners, and translation is often more art than science. For your edification and reading pleasure, here are notes on some of the places where we could have gone in a different direction in our translation of the work, or where a Japanese cultural reference is used.

Mochi, page 38

Mochi is a glutinous rice cake that is eaten all year round but is traditionally associated with the New Year holiday. It is baked, grilled, boiled, and eaten by itself or with other dishes.

Osechi Ryori, page 39

Osechi ryori is a special cuisine eaten during the New Year's holiday. *Osechi ryori* is akin to Thanksgiving dinner in that the leftovers are eaten for days afterwards.

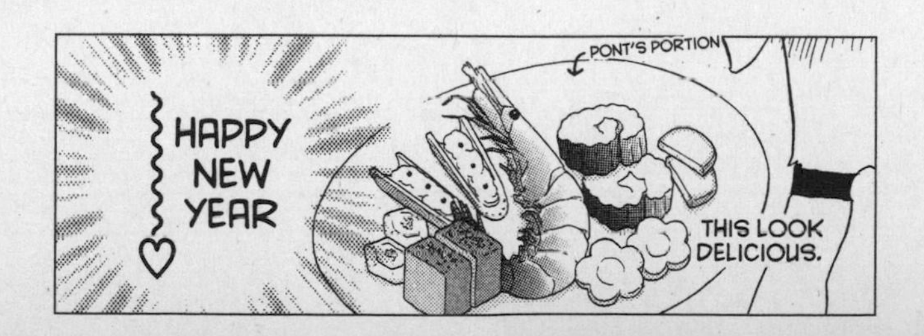

O-toso, page 40

O-toso is a spiced sake drunk during the New Year's holiday.

George Asakura, page 41

George Asakura is the popular manga artist who created Del Rey's *A Perfect Day for Love Letters*. These are her characters dressed up as the Kashimashi Musume, a trio of sisters who are performers in Japan.

© GEORGE ASAKURA♥♥♥

Kotatsu, page 43

A *kotatsu* is a low table with an attached electric heater and a blanket sandwiched between the table and the tabletop. People enjoy sitting under it during the winter.

Hatsumode, page 52

Hatsumode is the Japanese term for the first visit to a shrine or temple in the new year.

Ronin, page 64

Ronin were masterless samurai who took on freelance jobs to pay the bills. Nowadays, *ronin* refers to high school students whose grades aren't good enough to get them into a decent university, so they take a year off to study and take the test again.

The Kinki Kids, page 77

The Kinki Kids are a J-pop duo comprised of Tsuyoshi Domoto and Koichi Domoto (unrelated). Their ubiquitous songs and good looks have made them very popular in Japan, where they appear on several variety shows. Their name refers to the Kinki region of Japan, which encompasses Osaka, Kyoto, and Kobe.

Valentine's Day, page 84

Valentine's Day in Japan is a little different than it is here. Only women give chocolates or presents to the men they like, including friends and/or relatives. Men have their own day to give women presents/chocolate called White Day, which is one month later on March 13th.

Pin Pon!, page 91

Pin Pon is a phrase the Japanese use to signify you've hit the nail on the head. It comes from the sound used in game shows that signifies a correct answer.

Shabu Shabu, page 94

Shabu Shabu is a famous dish in Japan where thinly sliced meat is dipped in hot broth and eaten.

Dashimaki Eggs, page 96

Dashimaki eggs, a thin layer of fried eggs rolled into a sushi roll, are usually found in osechi ryori mentioned earlier.

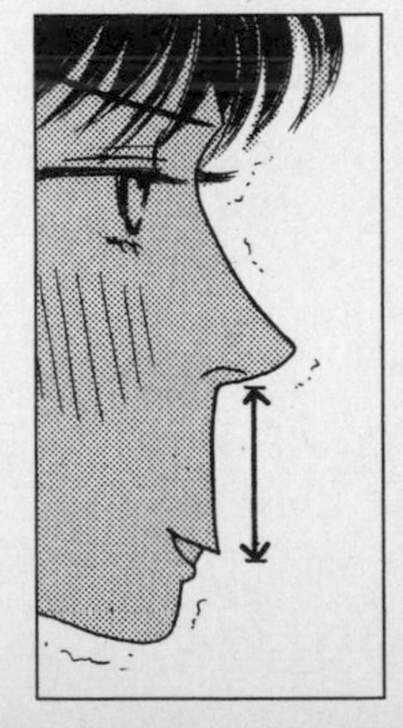

Under your Nose..., page 124

Notice how the space between Go's nose and lip seems to be stretching? This is a literal example of the Japanese phrase *Hana no shita ga nobiru* or, "the part under your nose is getting longer." It's used to describe someone head over heels in love or lust.

Gaster-10, page 136

Gaster-10 is an extremely popular over-the-counter drug that treats heartburn.

Pia, page 137

Pia is a guidebook that features information about restaurants, events, festivals, etc. for each region in Japan.

Ikebana, page 170

Ikebana is the traditional Japanese art of flower arrangement. Ike-Ponta would therefore be the traditional Japanese art of dog arrangement...

Doo-Doo?, page 179

In the original Japanese, the man uses the term *enkou*, which is an abbreviation for *enjokous*, or teen prostitute. Ponta, with her limited vocabulary, mistakes *enkou* for *unko*, the word for poop. *Enjokousai* refers to teenage prostitution, where a young, usually high school–aged girl "escorts" elderly men in order to get money for expensive items.

Love Hotels, page 186

Kyukei is the word for "rest" or "break," and at a love hotel—hotels in Japan where couples go for an intimate repose—it's akin to renting a room by the hour.

Preview of Volume 3

We're pleased to present you with a preview from Volume 3. This volume will be available in English on March 7, 2006, but for now you'll have to make do with Japanese!

ぐるぐるポンちゃん
「まいにちがぼうけん」の巻
生後2か月のポンちゃんはまいにちがぼうけんです
どれもおなじにみえるケド
コレがポンちゃん
まって〜〜〜え
とててててッ
ズボ
……

ぽて
……
えぐ…
マンマ〜〜
キューン キューン
キュンキュン
キュ…
ポツ
ポツ
ポツ
ザ———!…
カンベンしてよ
そのころママは
ふぇッ そんなモノたべちゃダメッ
アッ ホーキでかまないの
手いっぱいだった……
キュン キュン キューン
キュン キュン

あーあ こんなに 濡れちゃって
ハマッちまったのか
……あったかぁい……

ガサ…

ママのお迎えだ

どーもスミマセンでした

アリガト

バイバイ

いーえ

メッ

ゴメンナサイ…

でもネ ママ あのひと

すごぉくやさしかったンだあ……

未来くんとポンちゃん

じつはずうっと前に出逢ってたんだね…♡

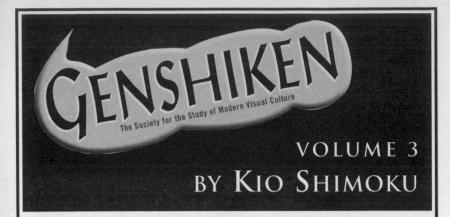

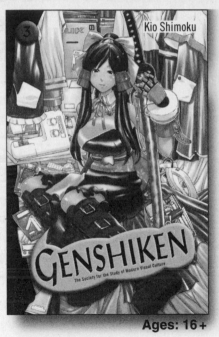

BY SATOMI IKEZAWA

Yaya Higuchi has a rough life. Constantly teased and tormented by her classmates, she takes her solace in dressing up as a member of her favorite rock band, Juliet, on the weekends. Things begin to look up for Yaya when a cute classmate befriends her. Her devotion to Juliet, however, eventually just brings her more of the teasing and harassment she gets at school. Unable to cope, Yaya . . . changes. Suddenly, Yaya is gone—and in the blink of an eye, a new personality emerges. She is now Nana and she is tough, confident, and in charge. Nana can do things that Yaya could never do—like beating up the boys and taking care of all of Yaya's problems. How will Yaya live with this new, super-confident alternate personality? Who will be the dominant one, and who is the REAL Yaya?

Ages: 16+

Special extras in each volume! Read them all!